the simple guide to FERRETS

Bobbye Land

t.f.h.

T.F.H. Publications, Inc.

© 2003

Distributed in the UNITED STATES to the Pet Trade by T.F.H. Publications, Inc., 1 TFH Plaza, Neptune City, NJ 07753; on the Internet at www.tfh.com; in CANADA by Rolf C. Hagen Inc., 3225 Sartelon St., Montreal, Quebec H4R 1E8; Pet Trade by H & L Pet Supplies Inc., 27 Kingston Crescent, Kitchener, Ontario N2B 2T6; in ENGLAND by T.F.H. Publications, PO Box 74, Havant PO9 5TT; in AUSTRALIA AND THE SOUTH PACIFIC by T.F.H. (Australia), Pty. Ltd., Box 149, Brookvale 2100 N.S.W., Australia; in NEW ZEALAND by Brooklands Aquarium Ltd., 5 McGiven Drive, New Plymouth, RD1 New Zealand; in SOUTH AFRICA by Rolf C. Hagen S.A. (PTY.) LTD., P.O. Box 201199, Durban North 4016, South Africa; in Japan by T.F.H. Publications. Published by T.F.H. Publications, Inc.

Library of Congress Cataloging-in-Publication Data
Land, Babs.
The simple guide to ferrets / Babs Land.
p. cm.
Includes index.
ISBN 0-7938-2116-9 1. Ferrets as pets. I. Title.
SF459.F47 L36 2003
636.976'628--dc22
2003017123

Contents

Part 1 – So You Want a Ferret" **9**

Ch. 1 – Should You Get a Ferret? 11

What is a Ferret? 12

Ferret History 13

"Thieves" 14

Ferret Ownership 15

Do Your Homework 16

Points to Ponder Page 20

Ch. 2 – Ferret Considerations 19

Legality 21

Time 22

Ferret Odor 23

Financial Issues 25

Travel 25

Ferrets and Children 26

The Multiple-Species Home 26

Socialization 27

lullaby Cradle

Ch. 3 – Where To Get a Ferret 31
        Where Can I Find a Ferret? 32
        Check the Conditions .38

Ch. 4 – Selecting the Right Ferret for You 41
        "Special Needs" Ferrets 42
        Check it Out 43
        Spaying and Neutering 45
        Ferret Colorations 46
        Ferret "Patterns" 48
        Age 50
        More Than One? 51
        Personality and Temperament 52

Before You Make a Deal Page 37

Part 2 – Caring for Your Ferret . . . .
Ch. 5 – Before You Bring Your Ferret Home 55
        Finding a Veterinarian .55
        Planned Ferret-Hood 58
        Food and Water Containers 60
        The Litter Box 61
        Bedding 62
        Ferret-Proofing Your Home 63

Ch. 6 – The Adjustment Period 71
        Children and Ferrets 72
        Patience 73
        Helping Your Ferret Adjust to His New Home 74
        Handling Your Ferret 75
        Ferret Introductions 77
        Introducing Your Ferret to Other Pets 78
        New Owner Misconceptions 80

Ch. 7 – Housing Your Ferret 85

A Free-Roaming Ferret? 85

Where to Get a Cage 87

What Goes in the Cage? 88

Cage Placement 91

Cage Cleaning 93

A Cage is a Must
Page 87

Ch. 8 – Feeding and Nutrition 97

How to Read Nutrition Labels 98

Feeding Time 100

Ferret Foods 101

Special Treats 103

The Obese Ferret 10

Feeding the Sick Ferret 10

Ch. 9 – Litter Box Training 111

Litter Box Habits 112

The Litter 113

Correcting Mistakes 114

Why Did My Ferret Stop Using the Litter Box? . . .115

Waste Management 117

Ch. 10 – Grooming Your Ferret 119

Does My Ferret Need a Bath? 119

Hard As Nails 123

Ear and There 125

Sink Your Teeth Into It 126

Part 3 – Your Ferret at Home **129**

Ch. 11 – Ferret Health Care 131
Vaccinations 132
Common Ferret Ailments 133
Other Health Concerns 140
Parasites 142
Home Health Care .143

Ch. 12 – Emergency Care for Your Ferret 145
Be Prepared 147
Emergency Problems and Solutions 148
Home Treatments .150
How to Plan for an Emergency 150
Possible Emergencies 153
Home Care 155
Disaster Emergency Tips 156

Ch. 13 – Ferret Behavior Problems 157
Defining Bad Behavior 158
Causes of Problems 160
Problems with Previously Owned Ferrets 161
Ferret Communication 163
Ferret Body Language 164
Sound Language 167

Ch. 14 – Traveling with Your Ferret 169
Pet Sitters 170
Boarding Facilities .171
Taking Your Ferret with You 174
Staying in a Hotel .175

Think Like a Ferret Page 159

Ferrets and the Law 176
Lost Ferrets 177

Ch. 15 – Caring for the Older Ferret 179
Feeding 179
Home Health Care 181
Expanded Veterinary Health Care 182
Cancers 183
Time to Say Goodbye .186

Ch. 16 – Ferret Rescue Organizations 189
Shelter Volunteers 190
Why Are So Many Ferrets Homeless? 192
Education is Key 193
Get Involved 195

Resources 197

Index 203

Home Health Care Page 181

Part One
So You Want a Ferret

"I want a pet that matches my personality, so which one of you likes candle light dinners, long walks on the beach, and is a non-smoker?"

Should You Get a Ferret?

If you are thinking about adopting a ferret, you're certainly not alone. According to a recent survey by the American Pet Products Manufacturers Association (APPMA), ferrets now officially rank as the third most-popular household companion pet in the US, and are outranked only by dogs and cats. It is roughly estimated that there are more than a million ferrets in the US today. This is especially noteworthy when you realize that the US pet trade only began seriously promoting the ferret as a household pet in the 1970s.

Even though ferrets are currently considered illegal in several states and cities, ferret ownership numbers are still skyrocketing as

The ferret is an increasingly popular pet in the United States.

more and more people discover the ferret's unique and charming personality. It is roughly estimated that there are more than a million ferrets in the US today.

The APPMA, a national group representing pet-supply manufacturers and importers, has conducted National Pet Owners Surveys since 1988. The APPMA's survey indicated that ferrets were owned in about six percent of the five million households owning small animal pets, excluding cats and dogs. Thus, approximately 300,000 households nationwide own ferrets. A similar survey conducted by the American Veterinary Medical Association (AVMA) supports these numbers. Because ferrets are illegal in many states, there were probably a lot of people who chose not to participate in the survey or did not answer the questions truthfully. Therefore, the actual number of ferrets in the US could feasibly be quite a bit higher.

What is a Ferret?

Even though many ferret owners teasingly refer to their ferrets as "weasels" this isn't true. Although they are cousins of the weasel (as well as otters, minks, badgers, wolverines, skunks, martens, mongooses, and raccoons– all members of the Mustelidae family), the ferret is a separate and distinct species. Although some people mistakenly believe that they are members of the rodent family, ferrets are true carnivores and cannot digest fibrous vegetables and fruits.

Some ferret owners lovingly but mistakenly call their pets "weasels."

Unlike our domesticated cats and dogs, the domesticated ferret is not, and has never been, a wild animal. A domesticated ferret cannot survive in the wild today. However, there are some species of ferret that do live in the wild. For example, Black-Footed Ferrets are found in some parts of the US and have been considered the most endangered mammal in North America for many years. They are considered more polecat than ferret, and are not believed to have even been part of the evolution of our domesticated ferret.

Ferret History

Scientific evidence, proven by blood tests conducted on the ferret, shows traces of ferrets descending from the European polecat. However, our domesticated ferrets bred to the European polecat do not make trustworthy pets, although it's interesting to note that the resulting offspring are more likely to be able to exist in the wild than our domesticated ferrets.

It's unclear exactly at what part of our history ferrets first appeared. Historians and ferret enthusiasts debate this question quite earnestly. According to historians ferrets were in existence as early as 600 A.D. In the Middle Ages in England, records show that "the ownership of ferrets is restricted to those earning 40 shillings (about $300) or more a year," which certainly proves that they not only existed, but were highly favored. Ferrets have been in America for more than 300 years,

Ferrets descended from polecats similar to this 37-day-old kit.

Appropriately Named

The name "ferret" comes from the Latin word *furo* meaning "thief," and what an apt name it is. The ferret operates on the assumption that if he sees something he wants, it should be his, no matter what.

Hunters once used ferrets for their burrowing abilities.

Ferrets like to take and hide things that they find around the house.

Centuries ago, biting was a desired ferret trait.

and in the 1800s they were imported in great numbers from New Zealand to aid in rodent control.

For centuries, domesticated ferrets were bred exclusively for use in hunting small animals, such as rabbits. Ferrets that are used for hunting are not supposed to actually catch the small animal. It is curiosity that drives the ferret into the rabbit hole, and it's the ferret's smell that drives the rabbit out. The hunter and the nets or guns do the rest.

"Thieves"

Ferrets love to explore and have been known to take things that they find around the house. No other pet that commonly shares a human household is as much of a thief as a ferret who sees something that he wants. He'll go after it immediately, even if it's something expressly forbidden him. Because ferrets are borrowers, you can be prepared to find their "loot" in places you might have thought inaccessible to them. One newbie ferret owner was shocked to find a handful of coins, a hairbrush, a stuffed toy, a few other assorted "treasures" that had obviously been stolen from a trashcan, and the car keys that had been lost for weeks–all inside a dryer vent hose that her thrifty ferret had not only managed to pull loose from the dryer, but also decided to use as a storage chest. Luckily, she had a sturdy cap over the dryer vent on the outside of her home, or her ferret could have easily made his way outdoors, where he would likely have been permanently lost.

Burrowing, hiding, biting, and most other behavior oddities of the ferret were what originally made them so attractive to their owners, who used them for hunting and

Problem Behaviors?

Although there are few true temperament problems in ferrets, some of their inherent behaviors are perceived by many as "problem behaviors." These problems require dedication on the part of the pet owner to work through them before they become out of control and develop into a behavior that you cannot live with. Remember that any problems you may perceive as "behavior" problems may just be a typical ferret displaying typical ferret behavior. The bottom line is that you should do your homework before you decide to share your home with a ferret.

There's a lot more to a ferret than cuteness.

later for rodent control. However, it is their cunning charm that has firmly ensconced them into society as a family pet.

Ferret Ownership

Even though they are easy to care for, ferret ownership is a much bigger responsibility than most people realize. Until they do their homework, many people think of ferrets as cute little "caged creatures" that they might enjoy having and watching, much as someone would keep a tank of colorful tropical fish. Living with a ferret that expects to be an active and interactive part of the family, instead of a caged bystander, can be a major shock to a new ferret owner who is unprepared for their charming, but sometimes mischievous antics, and for the responsibility associated with sharing his or her home with a ferret.

Expect to provide for your ferret's comfort.

Know a ferret up close and personal before buying him.

Ferrets are the perfect pets for the right person.

Ownership Responsibilities

A ferret is a living, breathing social creature that will not only want, but will also expect, to be accepted fully into the heart and home of his new family. That includes time spent outside the cage (several hours a day) as well as time spent inside his cage (which should be large, spacious, and tidy, and placed so as to make him feel like part of the family). You may find that one of the biggest decisions in purchasing a ferret is not only choosing the cage, but also deciding where to place it. A cage that's large enough to be comfortable for the ferret will take up quite a large chunk of space in any normal-sized room.

Just as you would for any other pet (or small child), you will be expected to provide for your ferret's every comfort, in addition to providing the basic care necessary to keep him clean, healthy, and fit for life. Unfortunately, a ferret's five- to ten-year expected lifespan is not as long as most dog's or cat's, but they pack so much life into those years that they are well worth the effort to keep them around (and happy) for as long as possible.

Owning any pet is a serious commitment, and it's certainly no different when you own a ferret. In fact, this commitment is even more serious because a ferret is not your usual family pet. A ferret operates on a wavelength that is like no other domesticated animal. People who own ferrets are quick to tell you that a ferret is not a pet for everyone, although they are the perfect choice for the right person.

Do Your Homework

It is vitally important that you do the proper homework before you make the choice to add a ferret to your household. Take the time to talk to breeders and other ferret owners and get to know as many ferrets as possible on an "up close and personal" basis. Don't be swayed by button eyes and a mischievous grin through the bars of a pet store cage. Ask questions, gather information, and make an informed decision that you're sure you can live with for the next five to ten years (the oldest ferret on record was 15 years old at the time of his death). Once you've decided that you want to be a ferret owner, your work has only just begun. Shop around. Visit as many breeders as possible, and check out pet stores and rescue shelters until you find the ferret that you immediately know was meant to share your home. When you've chosen that perfect ferret, and see it happily co-existing with other family members (animal and human), you'll know that you made the right choice. You are now officially a "ferret person."

Once you've made the decision to share your home and your heart with a ferret, your life will never again be the same. Buckle up and get ready for a life filled with laughs, smiles, and the occasional frustration. Your world will be enhanced by the addition of a ferret (or two, or three).

Ferret Considerations

Bringing any pet into your family requires a lot of careful consideration. However, making the decision to bring home a ferret brings on a completely different set of considerations along with the ones usually expected when adopting a new pet.

You should read everything you can find on the Internet, through various newsgroups, ferret mailing lists, and the many wonderful and informative ferret websites provided by national and local ferret groups, as well as individual ferret owners and breeders. You should also try to talk to as many longtime ferret owners, breeders, shelter volunteers and employees, pet store employees, and various local and national ferret

A pet is a lifetime commitment.

Points to Ponder

Before you bring home your ferret, run through this checklist of questions to ensure that you have thought of every angle of ferret ownership, and that you are truly ready to accept the commitment and responsibility of owning a ferret.

- Will I have an hour or more every day to spend with my ferret?

- Will I have time to take care of his daily needs, as well as spend quality time playing and bonding with him?

- Will I be able to afford the purchase price of the ferret and the necessary supplies (cage, bowls, litter pan) and the ongoing expenses (veterinary care, vaccinations, food, and litter)?

- Have I done enough research to realize the responsibility involved in day-to-day living with a ferret?

- Have I spent enough time with ferrets to understand their peculiar habits, as well as their unique smell, and know that these won't bother me?

- Will I still want a ferret once the "newness" has worn off and he is no longer a novelty?

- Do I truly want a pet for life and not just through its "cute stage"?

If you can answer each of these questions positively, then it's time to start looking for the right ferret for you!

Your pet needs a large, comfortable cage.

members as possible. Visiting a ferret shelter and speaking to the individual caretakers will provide the best information available. They have likely "seen it all" at some point, and can give you pointers to look for as "potential danger signals" when choosing your ferret. The more people you talk to and the more you read and learn, the better equipped you will be to make an informed decision about keeping a ferret for a pet. There are several factors to consider before you bring home a ferret–do all the research you can to make sure that you are able to handle the responsibilities of ferret ownership.

Before deciding on any pet, you should seriously consider what pet experts call "the commitment factor." You should never choose a pet on a whim, based on how cute he is, or how clever he seems. A pet is a lifetime commitment. (If not for your lifetime, certainly for the pet's lifetime.) Your new pet will depend on you for everything in his life including food, shelter, and love. Ferrets need daily attention in addition to having their basic nutritional and housing needs met. Be sure that you will still want the responsibility and will be able to honor the commitment you've made long after the "newness" has worn off, and the ferret has become just another member of the family.

Too many ferrets are purchased by people who have not done their research or have not spent time considering their decision to bring a new pet into their home. Many times, these ferrets, through no fault of their own, end up either being sorely neglected by owners who didn't have time to take on the responsibility of another living creature, are turned in to animal shelters or a ferret rescue organization, or worse yet, turned loose into the wild where they will die. Make sure that you don't add to the overcrowding in our nation's animal shelters, and be sure that you truly want the ferret you will be bringing into your home.

If you rent, make sure your lease allows ferrets in your building.

Legality

Before you get your heart set on a ferret, it is very important to find out whether or not it is legal for you to own a ferret where you live. In most areas, there are few laws (other than livestock and poultry laws) that govern what type of pet you may own except for the few city councils in various states that have established breed-specific laws to ban various dog breeds from residing within their city limits. There are entire states, however, that ban ferrets, and many cities have passed ordinances banning ferrets as pets within states that have no bans. If you or a family member serves in any of the armed forces, you should be aware that many military bases ban ferret ownership at the discretion of the base commander.

Ferrets require at least two hours per day outside their cage.

Some ferret owners scoop or change the litter every day.

Obviously these bans don't keep residents in those cities and states from owning a ferret (as proven by the many ferret clubs that exist in these localities and veterinarians that continue to provide medical care to ferret clients), but it does make it a bit more challenging to find good health care, food, supplies ,etc. for a forbidden ferret if the owner lives in one of those areas. Some landlords specifically refuse to have ferrets in their rental units, so check your lease contract agreement if you live in a rental house or apartment.

Because ferret lovers are constantly "fighting city hall" to promote the legalization of ferrets nationwide, it is impossible to keep a current list of cities and states that presently prohibit ferret ownership. Therefore, it is wise to check with your municipality about local or state ordinances before you purchase a ferret.

Time

You should also take into consideration whether or not you actually have the time available in your schedule to devote to a ferret. While they won't require the frequent walks that a dog would, and you won't need to schedule time for obedience school, ferrets certainly come with their own built-in time requirement factors.

You should also realize that your vacation plans might have to include the ferret. If you can't find a good house-sitter/ferret-sitter, or if you can't find a boarding kennel that accepts ferrets, your vacations will have to be planned around places that do accept your ferret, or you'll have to schedule day trips instead of planning to stay away overnight.

Can I Have a Ferret?

Make certain that ferrets are legal in your area before you decide to own one. They are illegal in some states, some larger cities, and some military bases. If you'd like to join the fight to make ferrets legal everywhere, your help will be greatly appreciated. The fight is localized on the two coasts, in California and New York City. For more information, you can write to:

Californians for Ferret Legalization

410 Mountain Home Road

Woodside, CA 94062

Website: www.ferretnews.org

The New York City Ferrets Association

Cathedral Station

PO Box 952

New York, NY 10025-0952 or at

Website: www.NYCFerrets.com

Both well-deserving groups will welcome your support in any way you can give it.

Although most people do keep their ferrets caged a great deal of the time, no one should purchase a ferret if they are not sure that they will have enough time to give the ferret free time to explore and play in a ferret-proofed area. Ferrets require a minimum of two hours per day outside their cage (many breeders and owners say that four hours a day outside the cage is necessary for a well-rounded, happy pet). Everyone agrees that the more time the ferret spends outside the cage with his humans, the better pet your ferret will become.

Besides the time actually spent socializing with your ferret, you will also have to allot the time necessary to take care of his daily maintenance. This will always include scooping out or completely changing his litter pan, giving him fresh food and water, as well as the weekly changing (and laundering) of the bedding, hammocks, and toys.

Ferret Odor

Because ferrets are related to skunks and weasels, you can probably guess that they emit a musky odor. This smell is milder than a skunk's and is tolerable to most people, especially if you take the proper steps to reduce it. Many owners do not mind this smell, and some people become used to it just as people who have cats and dogs rarely notice the odors associated with those pets.

No matter how fastidious you are about keeping your ferret, as well as his cage, litter box, and bedding clean, you cannot completely eliminate the unique odor of a ferret. Before

Wash and change your pet's bedding at least once a week

A monthly bath is usually sufficient

purchasing a ferret, you must ask yourself whether or not you (and the other members of your family) can tolerate the smell of a ferret. If the answer is yes (and it is for most people), then a ferret may be a good choice of pet for you. If your answer is no, then a ferret would not be such a good idea, and you should consider adopting another pet.

One of the most effective ways of reducing a ferret's odor is to invest in an odor-eliminating spray. This can be sprayed in the litter box, on the bedding, and with some products, directly on the ferret's fur. Always follow the directions on the product's label to avoid harming your pet.

Another very successful method of reducing odor is to replace the ferret's bedding often. If you notice that the sleep sack or blanket is getting dirty, remove it from the cage and wash it. Don't purchase anything for a ferret to sleep in or on that isn't washing machine safe. Most ferret owners have an extra set of bedding so that while one set is being washed, they have another to replace it with. The bedding should be changed at least once every week, but more often is better.

If your ferret has not been descented, you should see your vet about having the procedure done immediately, not only because non-descented ferrets can have medical problems involving the scent glands, but also because it will decrease any odor problem immensely.

How often you bathe your ferrets also contributes to the amount of odor they have, although if they are bathed too often they will actually have more of an odor than a ferret that is not bathed at all. This occurs because the skin dries out and the scent gland needs to work extra hard to replace the oils that are lost. It may take a few days after a bath for your ferret to start smelling normal again. Unless your ferret has gotten into something sticky or dirty, a monthly bath is usually sufficient.

Financial Issues

You should also consider the monetary aspect of taking on the responsibility of another living creature that will need daily maintenance, food, vitamins, treats, bedding, and toys for stimulation. With ferrets, toys are a necessity, not a luxury. A bored ferret quickly becomes a destructive ferret, and he may exhibit behavior problems that you might find unacceptable. Your ferret will also need annual vaccinations and medical checkups and may require emergency veterinary care. All of these things may seem nominal at first, but they do add up. Be sure that you can afford to give your ferret all the necessary care he will need throughout his lifetime.

Travel

Do you travel often? If so, are you willing to limit traveling away from home for more than a day trip unless you can find a boarding kennel that accepts ferrets, or can find a good ferret-sitter? Unlike cats, ferrets cannot be left alone for a weekend or for a few days without supervision. Ferrets need daily socialization, playtime, and free time out of the cage. If you travel, do you know someone who will be willing to take care of your ferret while you are out of town? Many boarding kennels will not board ferrets, and some house and pet-sitters will not accept ferret-owning clients. Be

For ferrets, toys are a necessity, not a luxury.

Annual physicals will help keep your pet healthy.

A Happy Home

You will have to provide your ferret with a large, comfortable cage where he can spend his time. A ferret's cage should never be used as punishment for any indiscretion. It should be a happy place for him, filled with interesting toys, comfortable bedding, food and water, and placed in a location where he will feel like part of the family even when he is not running loose with his humans.

Children and ferrets can be excellent companions.

sure before you bring a ferret into your home that you can easily make arrangements for his or her care while you are away on business or vacation.

Ferrets and Children

Do you have, or are you planning to have, children? Children and ferrets can be excellent companions. But unless the ferret has been raised with children, the louder voices and more frenetic actions of the average child may frighten the ferret, at least until he gets used to his new home. It will be very important to limit the interaction between your children and the ferret until you are sure that they understand each other.

Common sense should tell you that no infant should be left alone with any pet no matter how well trusted the pet is. Although a ferret isn't likely to harm a small child on purpose, the ferret can inflict damage to the child's tender skin with his teeth or nails, simply in trying to entice the child to play, or when trying to be friendly.

Children who are taught from the beginning that the ferret is not a plaything and must always be treated with respect, kindness, and affection, should do quite well in sharing their home with a ferret. However, unless you are prepared to scold the child in some circumstances where the ferret has misbehaved as a direct result of the child's actions, you should reconsider getting a ferret until your children are older. Children and ferrets should have a mutual respect for each other, but this is only possible with positive reinforcement from the adults in the family.

The Multiple-Species Home

It's not just the human family members that should be taken into consideration when deciding if you truly want to share your home with a ferret. If your home is one with other pet species (a dog, cat, or another household pet), it's important to take each of the other pets in the household into consideration when deciding whether a ferret will make a good addition to the home.

Someone who has Dachshunds or sighthounds (dogs that hunt game by sight, not smell) might want to reconsider bringing an animal into the home that could be considered a natural prey for his or her dogs. It isn't fair to the ferret or the dogs. Someone who breeds fancy hamsters, mice, or rats should not expect to be able to have the ferret (bred for centuries as ratters and mousers) and the rodents co-exist happily. Many cats and ferrets get along quite well, as do some breeds of dog, but you should always carefully socialize your new ferret with the family pets before allowing them within reaching distance of each other.

Socialization

Proper socialization procedures can prevent (or cure) many perceived behavior problems. The more your ferret gets to know and interacts with the people and other pets that you care about, the faster he will become an integrated part of your family.

Most ferrets are so inquisitive that they will enjoy meeting new people and other animals. While most people fear that their ferret will either harm or be harmed by their other pets, there's a good chance that

The Descenting Myth

Just because your ferret has been descented doesn't mean that he will not have an odor. Ferrets are members of the skunk family, and although their scent certainly cannot be compared to a skunk's spray, they have a slightly musky odor, even in the cleanest of situations. You can use baby wipes on your ferrets before company comes to make them a little "fresher" smelling for the noses that aren't accustomed to their unique body odor.

Some dogs get along well with ferrets if properly introduced.

they will become fast friends if the introduction is handled correctly. An added bonus in the cross-species interaction will be the entertainment value you'll receive when your cat or dog starts playing ferret games.

When introducing your pets to the ferret (and vice versa), it is of utmost importance that you strictly supervise the initial meeting. It's a good idea to have your dog on a leash or your cat firmly held until you can gauge their reactions to this new musky-smelling interloper to their territory.

Patience

One of the most important things a new ferret owner can provide is patience. If you don't have a lot of patience for training and behavior modification, you might want to consider getting a different pet. If your ferret starts nipping at you, or can't seem to remember where his litter pan is located, or turns into a finicky eater, you will need a double dose of patience, mixed with an abundance of love.

No matter how well your pets seem to get along, they should never be allowed together unsupervised. The most well meaning dog can easily get too involved with a game of chase or wrestle and accidentally wound or even kill his ferret friend. If the games start to get too rough between your ferret and other pets, it's time to have a "time-out" until all parties have calmed down. If the initial introduction is handled correctly, everyone in the household should get along fine and become one big happy family.

Although there are many factors to consider before you decide to bring home a ferret, the pros of ferret ownership certainly outweigh the cons. Ferrets are social, loving animals that

Does Everyone Want a Ferret?

Sometimes when a ferret is purchased as a pet for a child, the child grows weary of taking care of the pet, and it will be left up to a parent or older sibling to take over the responsibilities of the ferret's daily care. Are you sure that everyone in the family realizes the commitment necessary to having a ferret in the house? Is everyone willing to pitch in from time to time to help with the daily chores? Does anyone in the family have a problem with the purchase of a ferret? These questions need to be seriously addressed before the purchase is made. It's too late afterward, when the ferret is sitting hungry and lonely in a dirty, smelly cage, to consider that perhaps no one in the family realized how much work was involved and no one is willing to commit to taking responsibility for the added duties.

Getting Along

Teach all children that a ferret is a living, breathing creature with feelings and that it is never acceptable behavior to hurt or to scare him. No matter how well they seem to be getting along, young children should never be left alone with a ferret, for the safety of everyone.

make great pets–for the right person. Once you have done all your research on ferret keeping and have decided that a ferret is the perfect pet for you, you can start looking for your new ferret friend.

Ferrets are social, loving animals that make great pets.

Where to Get a Ferret

There are many places to find a ferret including pet shops, breeders, the Internet, ferret rescue organizations, and advertisements in the local newspaper. Before you rush out and buy the first ferret you find, you should weigh all the pros and cons of where you are obtaining your ferret from before you make a decision. No matter where you find available ferrets, make sure that you are getting one that you can live with for his or her entire life. It's not fair to any animal to allow it become accustomed to a home, only to pass it along to someone else when the "newness" wears off or you decide that you don't have time for the ferret after all, or if you find that you've chosen a ferret with behavior traits that are unacceptable. Know

Get a ferret you can live with for his entire life.

The AFA

The American Ferret Association (AFA) offers many resources of places to find a ferret (breeders, rescue groups, etc.), and how to prepare for it, care for it, and help protect the species. You can contact them at:

The American Ferret Association, Inc.

PMB 255

626-C Admiral Drive

Annapolis, MD 21401

Phone: 1-888-FERRET-1

Website: www.ferret.org

Email: afa@ferret.org

Breeders know their ferrets as individuals

what you're purchasing before you bring the ferret home and make sure that the place of purchase has a good return policy in case of unforeseen personality conflicts or unexpected medical problems.

Where Can I Find a Ferret?

There are several places to find ferrets just waiting for a good home. Some of your options for purchasing a ferret include the following.

Ferret Breeder

By doing a search on the Internet for "ferret breeder" you can likely find a breeder within driving distance of your home. This breeder should be devoted to breeding good-quality ferrets and likely show them in competition. She should be very aware of what the different standards entail, and she should be breeding for good temperament as well.

Buyer Beware!

Any seller who is unwilling to answer your questions about ferrets or fails to understand the reasoning behind your queries should be avoided. If the ferret seller will not allow you to see the conditions under which the ferret is living, you should take your business elsewhere.

If she is truly serious about ferrets, she will likely be an excellent source of information about what you can expect from your ferret, and what your ferret will expect (and should receive) from you. Don't be surprised if she grills you thoroughly about what kind of home you'll be offering one of her babies. Remember, she has put a lot of time, thought, effort, and money—as well as love—into producing these little furry fellows. She just wants to be sure that she is sending the ferret off to a forever home where he will be happy and loved for the rest of his life, and, in turn, be able to provide his new owner with equal amounts of happiness and love.

The ferret breeder should be able to answer all of your questions and she should be willing to show you how and where her ferrets are housed and raised. All cages should be clean and as odor-free as possible. Litter pans should be clean and the cages should be tidy. Adequate bedding should be provided in each cage. The cages should be roomy and filled with interesting toys to keep the ferret entertained.

The primary reason for choosing a breeder is that she will know each ferret she owns on an individual basis, and she will likely be very anxious to match the right ferret with the right home. She won't send a quiet, sedate ferret into a home with young children, and she won't send a frisky youngster home with an elderly couple that wants a quiet companion. This breeder will also know the genetics behind each ferret she breeds, and will be willing to share with you any genetic health concerns that you should be aware of and watchful for.

Breeder Advantage

A ferret breeder probably will have already had her pets descented and spayed or neutered before she offers them for sale. If not, she will be able to recommend when it should be done. Remember that it can be costly to have these surgeries done, and this is a fact that should be taken into account when considering your purchase price.

A ferret obtained from a breeder should be roughly the same cost as one sold by a retail provider. The breeder may also have older ferrets available at a lesser price. A breeder will usually offer a health guarantee and will be available to help you work through any problems that might arise with your pet. She will likely have a good selection of males and females in various color patterns and ages.

The Pet Store

Almost every larger city or town will have at least one pet store that will have ferrets available or will let you special order them. Pet shops in large metropolitan areas will most likely have a larger selection of available ferrets at any given time, and will probably have a variety of colors and ages in both sexes. Pet shops have the added benefit of offering cages, supplies, and foods all in the same location where you purchase your pet, and may offer special bonus packages with the purchase of an animal.

Many pet stores offer guarantees and will replace any animal that is diagnosed with a current health problem within a certain length of time. Most pet store employees and clerks are very well educated regarding the types of animals they sell, and what their special needs are. They should have been able to observe the ferrets for at least a short period of time and may be able to advise you on what personalities and behaviors the different ferrets are displaying.

It is a good idea to get a health guarantee when buying your ferret.

Some large chain stores have veterinarians on staff, so you can possibly get a health checkup before you complete your purchase. Be sure you get a written statement that your new ferret has been descented and sterilized. If a female ferret has not been sterilized, be sure that the pet store will guarantee that she has not been caged with male ferrets and that there is no chance that she is pregnant. The area in which the ferrets are being housed should be clean and as odor-free as possible. There should be adequate numbers of litter pans for the number of ferrets being caged or housed together, and the litter pans should be clean. The bedding should be clean and tidy, and there should be lots of fun things to keep any active ferret entertained.

Local Animal Shelter

Sometimes, regular animal shelters in larger metropolitan areas will take in ferrets as well as the usual dog and cat turn-ins. They may ask for a nominal adoption fee, which will be considerably lower than the retail price of a ferret. The downside to such an adoption is that you will have to rely strictly on what you see. Shelter workers will likely not be able to tell you much beyond when the ferret was turned in, why the previous owner didn't want the ferret (and be aware that you sometimes cannot trust what a previous owner had to say about their pet), and what they have observed during the ferret's time with them. You will get no guarantees as to age, health, vaccinations or health records, and when you leave with the ferret, he is yours. If you have other ferrets, it will be especially important to keep this ferret quarantined from the rest for a period of time to make sure that he is not harboring any contagious diseases or illnesses.

Shelters and rescue groups may offer adult ferrets.

Ferret Rescue Organizations

An online search will bring up a large number of legitimate ferret rescue organizations across the country. While you may not always have a broad selection of color, sex, or age, it's amazing how many ferrets end up homeless each year through no fault of their own. Most rescue groups will have an application form for you to fill out, letting them know that you have done your homework, you know what you're getting into, what you expect from your new ferret, and what kind of home you can offer. Don't be insulted by their questions. Remember, these people are seeing firsthand every day how the very best

Learn all you can about a rescued pet's past.

Know what you're buying before you bring the ferret home.

intentions of a pet-buyer can quickly go awry at the first sign of a problem. They want to make sure that the ferret that has been entrusted to them goes to a home that is prepared to be a home forever.

When you visit the home of the foster parent or the rescue worker, you should find your prospective ferret in clean surroundings as described earlier, happy, healthy, and active. You should be given a vaccination record and a good description of what the foster person has observed during his or her time with this ferret. You may not be offered every ferret they have available. Trust the rescue person to know what he or she is doing. Rescue volunteers are true ferret professionals, and they will do their best to match the right ferret with the right home. They want to make sure that you are going to be happy with your new family addition, but also want to make sure that the ferret will be happy as well.

You will probably be charged a fee for a ferret from a rescue group or person, but in many cases it is more of a donation than a price tag. These people take in many ferrets that cannot be placed in new homes. The costs for taking in these unwanted ferrets is staggering, and the fees they charge for the ferrets that they are able to place doesn't come near to covering their annual costs.

If the rescue group is a non-profit organization, you might want to consider making a charitable donation if you're looking for a good cause. It will not only make your heart warm, but it's also a tax write-off. (Chapter 16 discusses ferret rescue organizations in depth and provides more information about how you can help neglected or unwanted ferrets.)

An Ad in the Newspaper

Many pet owners will try to place their animals themselves instead of turning them into a shelter or rescue network. Many times, they will offer not only to sell the ferret, but his cage and all his other supplies as well. If the ferret has not been abused in this home, does not have major temperament issues, and the owners have a legitimate excuse for getting

Before You Make the Deal

No matter where you obtain your ferret, be sure to get as much information in writing as possible about your new pet. Not only will your veterinarian need much of this information, but if something goes wrong later, it will help your case if you have proof that the ferret was not what it was said to be at the point of sale. Questions you should ask include:

·How old is the ferret? Was he or she bred by a pet supplier or by a local breeder?

·How long has the ferret been weaned and what type of food do they recommend? How many times a day is the ferret being fed now?

·Has the ferret been checked by a veterinarian? Can you have a copy of the veterinarian's report? (If a guarantee of health is offered, make certain to get a written copy.)

·Has the ferret been spayed or neutered? Is it descented?

·Has the ferret been housed with ferrets of the opposite sex? (This is very important if the ferret has not been spayed or neutered.)

·Is the ferret litter box trained? What kind of litter do they use and recommend?

·Has the ferret shown aggressive or submissive/shy tendencies toward other ferrets?

·Has the ferret shown aggressive tendencies to humans or other animals?

rid of him (allergies, moving, etc.), this could be an excellent opportunity for you. However, be aware that many times this is just an owner's way of getting rid of a problem. Be sure that you're not buying a health problem that is going to cost you, or a temperament problem that you may find too hard to deal with as a first-time ferret owner.

Ask to talk to the veterinarian that has treated the animal (the owner will likely have to ask the veterinarian to do so, as it is a breach of ethics for any vet to discuss an animal with you that does not belong to you) as well as talking with the current owner. Spend as much time as possible with the ferret, watching him in his

Watch out for cages that might be overcrowded.

No matter where you get your pet, check the cage and litter pans for signs of illness.

Ask the seller how long your ferret has been with his group.

cage, running loose in the house, and interacting with his humans to get an idea of his personality and temperament.

Check the Conditions

No matter where you find your ferret, he should be in a clean cage that is large enough for him, with proper toys and bedding. His litter pan should be fairly clean (check his litter pan to see if there are any signs of diarrhea), his food dish should be full, and he should have an adequate water supply. This is a signal that the current owner is knowledgeable about a ferret's needs and will more likely answer any questions you have.

If the ferret you choose is housed with multiple ferrets, check each ferret closely for signs of illness, not just the one ferret you are interested in. Ask how long this ferret has been with this particular group, and where he was housed before. If he just arrived at this facility within the past few days, ask if you can put him on hold, and come back to pick him up a few days to a week later. This should allow time for him to show any signs of stress or illness, or for the incubation period for any disease he might have been exposed to during shipment to manifest itself.

When you are searching for your ferret, you may notice that many breeders and pet shops care for their ferrets very differently. Be sure you choose your ferret from a supplier that truly cares about the animals they sell. Don't be swayed into purchasing a ferret that is being kept in inhumane conditions. Instead, report the situation to the local humane society and keep looking for an appropriate pet. A ferret that has been abused, mistreated, or has been housed incorrectly may have temperament and health issues that can be overwhelming to a new pet owner. Choose your ferret from conditions that are:

Part 1

• clean and as odor-free as possible

• well equipped with not only food and water, but also with sleep/snuggle sacks, hammocks, chew toys, and other interesting playthings

• under-crowded. Beware of any situation that has too many ferrets housed in a too-small enclosure

• safe. Carefully check before purchasing to see that the ferret you have chosen doesn't have scratches, bite marks, or puncture wounds from being kept in an unsafe enclosure, or from being kept with a more dominant ferret that abused it.

No matter where you decide to purchase your ferret, make sure that he is exhibiting no signs of illness, that he does not nip at you for any reason, and that he is being kept in clean, sanitary conditions. Be sure you get a health guarantee in writing, if it is offered, and make arrangements to take the ferret to the veterinarian for a well-pet checkup to be sure that he isn't harboring any health problems or parasites. Be sure to ask what long-term support, if any, is available in case you run into unexpected problems in the future.

Examine the pet you choose for bite marks and other damage.

The seller should always be available if you have problems with your ferret.

Selecting the Right Ferret For You

You'd think that doing your homework and making the big decision to purchase a ferret would be the hardest parts of the process of getting a pet ferret. However, once you've made that decision, the hardest part still lies ahead. Choosing among the thousands of ferrets available to new homes across the US every week and finding the one (or two or three) specific ferret(s) that will suit you, your home, and family is the most difficult task of all.

Obviously, the top consideration should be the health of your new pet. Owning a pet is expensive enough in the best situations; taking on the added expense of a pet that already exhibits health problems shouldn't be an option.

It's important to select a ferret that appears healthy.

Part 1

A healthy ferret is alert and has bright, clean eyes.

A Healthy Ferret is a Happy Ferret

When choosing your family pet, make certain to pick the healthiest animal you can find. Ferrets are fragile creatures even in the best of situations. Bringing home a ferret that is already exhibiting health problems is asking for trouble.

Straight, whole, and very white teeth are important to ferret wellness.

"Special Needs" Ferrets

Although you may feel sorry for an ill or otherwise "needy" ferret, resist the urge to adopt him, especially if you are a first-time ferret owner. "Special-needs" ferrets may have hidden health problems and could make other ferrets in the household ill. These ferrets could require special medications or operations that could run into hundreds or thousands of dollars worth of veterinary bills.

Choose a ferret that appears to be healthy, and take it to the vet to make sure that it doesn't just appear healthy, but that it is healthy. Have the vet do a complete physical on the ferret just to be sure that everything is okay. If your ferret doesn't get a clean bill of health from the vet, return to the place of purchase (where hopefully you obtained a health guarantee) and see about getting a replacement ferret or a refund.

It's Normal

Physiological values for healthy ferrets are as follows:

The average life span for a ferret is five to ten years (records show ferrets living as long as 15 years, but this is uncommon).

Sexual maturity occurs at five to nine months of age.

The gestation period is 41 to 42 days.

A ferret's eyes open between 21 and 37 days.

The weaning age is six to eight weeks, with eight weeks being preferred.

A ferret's normal body temperature is 100° to 103°F.

The ferret's gastrointestinal transit time is three to four hours.

The normal heart rate is 180 to 250 beats per minute.

Don't fall for the sales ploy that a ferret needs a "special home." Even though it tugs at your heartstrings, walk away from any special-needs ferret.

Check it Out

When evaluating the health of your potential pet ferret, be sure to check the following.

The Eyes, Ears, Teeth, and Nose

No matter what his age, your new ferret should be alert and active with clear, bright, clean eyes. There should be no drainage, tearstains, or mucus around the corners of the eyes. When selecting your ferret, it is very important to be aware of what constitutes a healthy ferret. The teeth should be straight, whole, and very white. There shouldn't be any buildup of tartar, especially if the ferret is very young.

A moist nose without any signs of illness is acceptable.

Ferret fur is soft and shiny.

How Can You Tell if a Ferret is Sick?

A sick ferret won't want to be bothered by you, his owner, or the other ferrets. He may show signs of an upper respiratory infection (runny eyes or nose), and you might hear him sneeze. A ferret that has been sick for a while will be thin, and his hair will look dull and lifeless. He'll be listless and lethargic, and even though he may play at your sympathy, you will have to be realistic and keep looking for the right ferret for you—a healthy ferret.

Ferret nails are kept trimmed.

The ears should be clean inside and out, with no waxy buildup inside (an indicator of ear mites) and no flea dirt behind the ears. Rips and tears on the ears can indicate a ferret that has been in several fights, which could be an indicator of bad temperament toward other ferrets, or a sign that he's been housed in an overcrowded area.

The nose should be clear of any mucous, crusting, or drainage, although some moistness is acceptable.

The Nails, Whiskers, and Fur

The ferret's fur should be shiny, soft, and should not have any bald patches or clumps. Although the fur will have a slightly musky odor, the scent should not be stronger than usual. The toenails should have been kept trimmed, and the whiskers should be strong and straight.

A Matter of Personal Preference

Choosing the color and sex of your new ferret is strictly a matter of personal preference. Males (hobs or gibs) and females (jills or sprites) are slightly different in size. The head of the male will be rounder and broader than that of the female, who has a longer, tapered nose. Neither sex should ever resemble a rat. Males weigh about 3 to 5 pounds, with females weighing half that of males. Males generally measure about 16 inches in length, and females measure approximately 14 inches.

Males and females require the same size cage and the same amount of time to take care of them, so size really shouldn't be much of an issue when determining what ferret to purchase.

A dirty derriere can denote health problems.

The Anal Area

The anal area should be free of any feces, caked or fresh. A dirty bottom can be a sign of diarrhea or another health problem. A veterinarian should examine the ferret before any sale is concluded.

Spaying and Neutering

The ferret you adopt should be kept in clean, safe conditions, and if it is unsterilized, it should have been kept with other ferrets of the same sex to avoid an unplanned mating. It is very important to get your ferret spayed or neutered (as well as descented). It will be almost impossible to keep a male ferret that has not been descented and neutered as an indoor pet. Aside from the behavior problems that will definitely occur in a fully fertile male, the musky odor can be overwhelming.

To avoid unplanned mating, keep males and females apart.

Part 1

Many different colorations of ferret are bred in the United States.

Black sable ferrets have blackish-brown guard hairs.

A female that has not been spayed will possibly be less smelly, but you will have the problem of her estrus (heat) cycles, which can actually lead to aplastic anemia and death if she is not spayed or bred. A ferret female that comes into heat will stay in heat until she is bred. This can cause her to bleed to death.

Sterilization is of vital importance when choosing your ferret. Most major ferret breeders spay and neuter them at a very young age (sometimes before shipping the ferrets out to pet stores), so if you purchase your ferret from a pet store, the surgery may have already been done. If the ferret wasn't sterilized, you should have it done as soon as the veterinarian deems it possible.

If you purchased your ferret from a breeder, she can tell you if her pets have been sterilized; and if not, at what age it can and should be done. Be aware that in some areas, spaying and neutering ferrets can be quite costly. It should definitely be a consideration when making your purchase, unless money is no object to you. Because of the type of procedure involved, it generally costs less to neuter a male than to spay a female.

Ferret Colorations

There are many different colorations of ferret being bred in the US today. Sable is the most common, and cinnamon is the most rare, with a myriad of colors and patterns in between. Ferrets usually change colors with the seasons and are generally lighter in the winter than they are in the summer. Many ferrets "lighten" as they age, too. Different ferret organizations recognize different colors and patterns, but unless you're planning to enter your ferret in a show, the exact label isn't particularly important when you're choosing a ferret.

Here's a brief overview of the types and colorations of ferrets available. The American Ferret Association can provide you with more details on the genetics and color patterns in ferrets.

Sable

Sable ferrets have deep-brown guard hairs (the longer, coarser hair on top), with a lighter color undercoat. The black sable has more of a blackish-brown guard hair with preferably a white undercoat. No bib (chest marking) is allowed. Sable ferrets are the most common color, followed closely by the white group.

Albino

The albino ferret, as in any other mammal, is pure white with red eyes and a pink nose. A dark-eyed white ferret with very light eyes could possibly be confused with an albino. Both of these "whites" can actually range from a true snowy white to cream-colored, although most breeders agree that the whiter the color the better.

The albino ferret is pure white and has red eyes and a pink nose.

Deaf Ferrets

Deafness in ferrets, when not caused by trauma, infection, or medication, can be linked to genetics, specifically a color gene, called the Waardenburg gene. This gene is what gives a ferret white markings toward the head region. The increasing popularity of dark-eyed whites, marked whites, pandas, and blazes in the ferret world has increased the presence of deafness.

Usually a ferret that has Waardenburg syndrome not only has white markings on the head region, but usually has wider-set eyes than his hearing counterparts. The two most common ferret breeds to have deafness are blazes (badger-type markings of a white stripe down the middle of the head) and pandas (entire head and neck area are white/no mask).

This does not mean that every ferret with white on his head is deaf, but that ferrets with those markings (and the extra indicator of wider-set eyes) should be tested carefully before purchase or if behavior problems indicate that deafness might be a contributing factor.

White

A dark-eyed white (often called a black-eyed white) is a ferret with white guard hairs but eyes darker than the red of an albino.

Chocolate

The chocolate ferret, as the name implies, is the color of a chocolate candy bar. The chocolate ferret is described as dark to milk chocolate brown with a white to golden or amber undercoat and highlights. The chocolate color is a variation of the sable. The dilution is a result of a small change in the structure of the pigment molecule, and until recent years, the chocolate was called Siamese.

Champagne and Cinnamon

It is very easy to confuse a champagne ferret and a cinnamon ferret unless you see the two side by side. The champagne has tannish guard hairs with a slightly reddish tint. The cinnamon has light reddish-brown guard hairs. Since diet and environment can give a champagne ferret an unnaturally reddish look, make sure if you are offered a "cinnamon ferret" at an inflated price that it is truly a cinnamon, and not an altered champagne.

Panda-like markings identify the silver Panda ferret.

Ferret "Patterns"

There are also "patterns" within the different ferret colors that add to the diversity of the appearance of the species.

A dark- or black-eyed white pattern describes a ferret that has white to cream guard hairs mixed with colored hairs (of sable, black, champagne, chocolate, etc.) Colored guard hairs are not evenly displaced.

A dark- or black-eyed white striped refers to a white ferret that has colored guard hairs (of any of the solid colors mentioned previously) forming a stripe that goes up the back to the ferret's shoulders.

Fine Points describe a ferret that is marked, with a lighter body (white or cream) with points (legs and tail) of any of the darker colors. This color pattern will have little or no darker color on the ferret's back, with a thin distinct "V" mask. No bib is allowed.

Point/Siamese is a ferret whose body color and points show a distinct difference in color concentration. Body color is cream and points can be any color. Unlike Fine Points, more color is found on the ferret's back, and the color concentration between body color and points is less distinct (but still obvious). They must have a "V" mask, but it may not be as thin as the Fine Point's mask.

Roan ferrets will look much like a "blue tick hound" or a "belton setter" with white to cream guard hairs mixed with any of the colored hairs and evenly displaced throughout the body. Some refer to this as "salt and pepper" coloring.

The **bib** refers to a white to cream coloring starting from the ferret's chin and reaching to the ferret's chest. It's only a marking and does not affect the ferret's color or pattern classification.

A Blaze or Badger marking is a long white or cream stripe starting from the forehead, reaching to the back of the neck and possibly even down to the shoulders. The stripe should be thick and obvious. A thin line on the top of a ferret's head should not be referred to as a blaze. Blazes also usually have eye rings and can be of any self color.

Knee Patches or Knee Pads are white to cream hairs located in the area of the knees. This is only a marking and does not affect the ferret's color or pattern classification.

A Mitt ferret has four white feet with a body color of any solid color other than white. The body color should come down all the way to at least the top of the ankle area, but cannot pass the bottom ankle area on any of the four feet in order to be considered a true "Mitt." Ferrets with white coloring on only the toes cannot be referred to as Mitts.

Who Was That Masked Ferret?

If you are buying a kit, don't look for one with a mask. Only a fully adult ferret will have a complete mask. Kits grow a mask by growing white hairs in two small patches just below the ears. In time, the white gradually fills in across the eyes. Some ferrets only have full masks when they are in full winter coat, and others carry them season after season, although their mask will sometimes appear smaller in winter. Sometimes as ferrets get older, their masks will change color somewhat as extra gray hairs join the white.

A **Panda** can have any of the darker solid body colors, with a mostly white face, head, throat, and neck. While a few splotches of color are acceptable in this area, it is not desired, except for eye rings. The body color must be present starting at the shoulders for the ferret to be classified as a true "Panda."

Age

It's possible that you will be given a choice between adopting an adult ferret and adopting a young kit. Ferrets are considered adults when they are four to six months old. What age ferret would fit best into your household? Let's look at the advantages and disadvantages to owning each.

Kits

A kit will definitely be more lively and entertaining than an older ferret. Of course, even adult ferrets can still be likened to young kittens in their playful antics at times. If you are a first-time ferret owner, you may be less intimidated by a young ferret because it will be smaller.

On the other hand, it takes considerable time and effort to train a young kit. Kits need constant attention regarding their housetraining/litter box training, and you will have to be firm regarding too-rowdy play. A kit that is allowed to bite and nip during play will likely grow up to be an adult that may be hard to handle.

Adults

If an adult ferret has been well treated and doesn't display any distrust or fear of humans, then he can make a wonderful addition to the family. An adult is well past all the training stages and a youngster's mischievousness. Adult ferrets can come right into your home and become part of the family without all the extra attention being required to turn them into responsible members of society.

However, a ferret that has been abused and mistreated will come with his own extensive set of needs. However much your heart may tell you that this ferret needs your love and attention, walk

Ferrets are considered adults when they are four to six months old.

away and leave this one to the experts. Rehabilitating an abused ferret is time-consuming, can be physically dangerous, and sometimes everything you do will not be enough. Wait until the right ferret comes along. A ferret that needs you and wants you will do his best to make you happy that you chose him.

Another advantage to the adult ferret is that you know exactly what you're buying. You can see the finished product, as opposed to purchasing a kit that may be larger or smaller than it appeared, with a different coat color or pattern, and perhaps even a different temperament than expected.

Be sure if you are considering an adult ferret that you can receive a guarantee that he or she has been neutered or spayed and descented. If not, this will be an added expense, as well as a risk. Spaying and neutering is considered "routine" surgery, but any surgery to a ferret can be a health risk.

Age is Just a Number

Whereas most pets are considered babies until they're a year old, a 5-month-old ferret is considered an adult and should be started on adult foods. On this same scale, a 3-year-old ferret is entering middle age, and a 5-year-old ferret is considered a senior citizen, and should have his food altered accordingly.

It will usually be less expensive to purchase an adult ferret. Most kits will be full retail price, whereas an adult may be available through rescue or purchased second-hand from a previous owner at a reduced cost.

The decision of which ferret to bring home will likely end up being a result of which ferret chooses you, or which one you fall in love with. If it's a kit, you know you'll have a great experience "growing up" together. If it's an adult, you can be amazed at how quickly he or she will adapt to you as if you had raised him or her yourself, and you'll avoid all the training problems.

More Than One?

You may find that ferret ownership is like eating potato chips–you can't have just one. Another choice you may be faced with is whether you want to purchase one ferret or more. Ferrets are social creatures and will definitely appreciate having a "partner in crime." One ferret can certainly be happy, if his humans give him enough toys and social stimulation. However, if you work during the day, or are gone from home frequently, you

Some people find they like to own more than one ferret

might want to consider purchasing two ferrets together, so you don't have to worry about one being left alone and lonely.

Don't think that you have to choose littermates or ferrets that have been caged together. After a brief socialization time, the average ferret will quickly adapt to having a strange ferret roommate and soon you'll find them snoozing together in their hammock, or playing together and sharing their toys.

If you adopt adult male ferrets, make certain that they both have been neutered. An adult male may become so territorial that he might kill any other ferret that shares his cage.

Personality and Temperament

Although all ferrets display a lot of the same merry affability, just like humans, individual ferrets will display slightly different personality and temperament traits. Beware of any ferret that appears afraid, timid, or even worse, attempts to nip or bite. Such behavior is unacceptable, and you should never consider adding such a ferret to your family.

While kits haven't developed their full personality at the eight to ten weeks of age when you'll likely be meeting them, you can get a good idea of their adult temperament. If a kit likes to cuddle, chances are that he'll always be a bit of a couch potato. However, if a kit is a squirming bundle of energy, be sure that you're prepared to bring a cute dose of trouble into your home.

There is no secret to choosing the perfect ferret. Once you have ascertained that the ferret you like is healthy and emotionally sound, the rest is simply a matter of personal preference, or waiting until the right ferret decides that you are the right person. The rest will be family history!

Part Two
Caring for Your Ferret

"Junior, for the last time! The litter box is not the beach! Now go take a bath!"

5

Before You Bring Your Ferret Home

Just as you wouldn't consider bringing a new human baby home from the hospital without having first purchased a crib, blankets, formula, clothes, and all the other necessary items, you should never bring home a ferret until you know that your home is going to be a safe, comfortable haven for your new pet, and that you have obtained everything required to provide for all his needs.

Finding a Veterinarian

The first thing to do before you bring your ferret home is to find a good veterinarian in driving distance of your home. Within 72 hours of arriving at your home, your ferret should go in for a "well-pet" exam and to complete the

You want your ferret to live in a safe, comfortable haven.

Choose your vet carefully. Your ferret's life is in her hands.

vaccination schedule that the breeder should have already begun.

Ask around when looking for a vet. Talk to other ferret owners in your local area, or a ferret shelter operator who can recommend a good vet. Be sure that the veterinarian you've decided on is not only available to ferret clients, but is also knowledgeable about the specific medical care necessary for ferrets.

Choose the vet carefully. Your ferret's life is going to be in this vet's hands many times during the years ahead. You should feel comfortable talking to the vet and the office personnel, and the vet techs should be friendly and knowledgeable. Find out how many ferret-owning clients the vet has and ask about his or her experience with ferrets. Some vets will not accept ferret patients and you may need to find an "exotics" veterinarian.

The Veterinarian

You should choose your ferret's veterinarian long before you bring your ferret home. A visit to the vet clinic without your pet is a good idea to see that you like the vet and the staff, and that you find the clinic clean and orderly. Make an appointment to talk with the veterinarian to ask about her credentials in treating ferrets. A dedicated vet will be honest with you if she does not have the proper experience and continuing education to treat your ferret, and she will be able to advise you of another clinic in your area where you should take your pet.

Be sure to find a vet that you can talk to, who you feel will listen to your ideas and suggestions and will understand that no one knows your ferret better than you do. It's important that you feel comfortable with the vet and her staff, since they will be the people screening her calls, relaying messages, and answering your phone calls. You owe it to your ferret to do the necessary research to make sure that the vet you choose is a capable one.

Ask Questions

When choosing your veterinarian, don't be afraid to ask the following questions.

√ How many ferret clients do you see? How often?

√ Do you have ferrets of your own?

√ What are your emergency call guidelines?

√ Will you come to the office anytime after hours in case of emergency? If not, where would you refer me?

√ Have you done continuing education regarding ferrets?

√ Do you keep up-to-date with ferret-specific medicine?

A nosy ferret is a healthy ferret.

The ferret you have purchased should have clear, bright eyes, an inquisitive nature, be alert and active, have adequately trimmed toenails, and have a glossy and thick coat (with allowances being made for seasonal sheds) that is soft to the touch. However, even a seemingly healthy ferret can be hiding symptoms of illnesses and disease. The first place your ferret should go is to your vet clinic to meet your veterinarian. While there, he should get a well-pet checkup to make sure that there are no hidden health problems, and get a baseline temperature and heartbeat reading for future reference. It's possible that he will need to receive vaccinations at this time. Be sure that you get a current health certificate, complete vaccination record, and a rabies certificate from the seller, whether you have purchased a young kit or an older ferret.

Make sure your curious pet is kept safe in your home.

Large cages have plenty of places for hammocks and sleeping tubes.

A Rose by Any Other Name

One of the most fun aspects of pet ownership is choosing the pet's name. You may want to wait until you have lived with your ferret for a few days before you choose a name, but it's always a good (and fun) idea to have some choices picked out ahead of time. Most ferrets don't really learn their names well, so you don't have to worry quite as much about a name for their sake. Unlike a dog, that learns to come when his name is called, a ferret will be more likely to come to a sound or a smell than a specific word.

Do a walk-through and make sure that the entire clinic is clean and orderly. Ask about clinic hours and emergency policies as well as payment policies. If the vet isn't available for emergencies, ask about an emergency vet in your area who is not only available, but who is also experienced with treating ferrets. You should also find a regular "backup" vet in case your vet is out of town or otherwise unavailable when you need her. Don't wait until the last moment; prepare in advance in case of emergency.

Planned Ferret-hood

There are many supplies that your ferret is going to need immediately, so it is best to purchase these items before you bring your ferret home. The better prepared you are, the smoother everything will go, and the more comfortable your new ferret will be. Your ferret will definitely pick up on your anxiety if you are scurrying around trying to prepare everything for him, and it will add to his already nervous state caused by being in a strange place with strange people.

The Cage

You will need to buy a cage in which to house your ferret when you are not home or for when the ferret will be unsupervised. The cage should be made of wire mesh, for better

Storing Your Ferret "Stuff"

One little ferret will need more paraphernalia than you'd ever expect. From treats and toys to food bags and medicines, the area on top of the ferret's cage can soon start to look messy. Purchase a good organizer tray to keep all the smaller items neatly tucked away. Attach a couple of legal-sized paper holders (found in any office supply store) to the side of his cage for keeping extra newspapers handy. Put the ferret's food in a plastic canister with a tight-fitting lid to keep it from spilling or from getting stale. This little trick will also prevent your ferret from chewing through the food bag.

ventilation, and should have at least two levels. Aquariums are never acceptable housing for a ferret, as they do not provide enough ventilation. Poor ventilation will make your ferret sick and make him feel isolated, which will prompt him to exhibit behavior problems.

You should also purchase a smaller carrying cage for vacations, day trips, or trips to the veterinarian. This cage should be kept equipped with its own water bottle, food dish, bedding, and litter pan, to be ready for unexpected emergency trips.

A wood cage is not a good choice for a ferret because the ferret is likely to destroy or damage it with his teeth and nails. The wood will also absorb any litter box accidents and odors, which will make it very difficult to keep the cage clean.

Cage Size

What size cage you purchase depends on how much time the ferret will be spending in the cage. If the ferret will be out running around most of the time, a smaller cage will be sufficient. If the ferret will be caged for any length of time, a cage 2 feet x 3 feet x 3 feet or larger should be used. The bigger the cage, the more room the ferret will have to stretch his legs. The cage should have at least two levels so that the ferret can have his sleeping area away from the litter box and the food area. The more levels available in the cage, the better physical condition your ferret will be in, because of the extra exercise he will get climbing around and playing in the cage. A large cage also gives you places to hang hammocks and tubes that your ferret will enjoy snoozing in.

The Cage Floor

Although wire cages are good for ventilation, having your ferret walk on a wire floor is not acceptable. Wire mesh is hard on a ferret's feet, so if you choose a cage with a wire bottom, you will need to cover part of the floor with towels, sheets, blankets, linoleum, or carpet remnants to protect the ferret's paws.

Use ceramic, not plastic, food bowls so that your ferret can't chew on them.

Ferret Food

Find out what brand or type of foods your ferret was eating at the breeder's or at the place where you obtained him. Buy some of the same food and keep your ferret on that diet until he has settled into his new home.

When purchasing a cage, check to make sure that it is sturdy and put together well. Also check for sharp edges that could hurt your ferret. Check that you can reach into all parts of the cage so that you can easily clean the cage and so you can get a hold of a frisky ferret that wants to play. (Cages and housing are discussed in more detail in Chapter 7.)

Food and Water Containers

Once you've decided on the proper cage, it's time to equip it. You will need to have a very heavy food dish for your ferret. Plastic dishes are easily tipped over and they're often used as a chew toy (which can be dangerous for your ferret). Ceramic crocks are excellent choices, especially if they can be attached to the wire sides of the cage.

Ferrets need access to cool, fresh water all the time.

Do not buy a small food bowl just because you have a small ferret. A dish that is 4 to 6 inches in diameter is about the right size. You might also consider checking out the bird supply aisle of your local pet store for large bird food dishes. They usually have a means of securely attaching to the side of the cage and are heavy and chew-proof as well.

All ferrets should have access to cool, fresh water at all times. You should buy a gravity-fed water bottle for your ferret's cage. Almost any size water bottle will do, but a 16-ounce size is just about right. Most water bottles will have a small amount of leakage, so it is a good idea to either place a heavy ceramic dish underneath it, or place the water bottle over the edge of the litter area. Some of the newer bottles are easily filled without taking the bottle off the cage (the top pops up and then reseals) and they seem to be more leak-proof than other types.

Extra Water

During hot summer months, keep a large crock of cool water available for your ferret besides his usual drip water bottle. Ferrets don't adapt well to hot weather, and if your house isn't air conditioned, a bowl of water will give your ferret a way to cool himself off.

Touring the Store

Shopping for your ferret should take you onto other aisles in the pet store besides the section reserved for ferret supplies. Many food and water dishes that are designed for use in birdcages will work equally well for your ferret, since they were made for critters that like to chew and toss around their dishes.

Treats for hamsters, rabbits, and cats will be equally tasty to your ferret. Cat toys are usually quite interesting to a ferret as well (although be careful when making your choice, because ferrets are usually quite a bit more destructive than the average cat). When you're in a large department store, check out the baby section for indestructible toys, too. These usually have rattles and bells inside that will fascinate your ferret.

Some people give their ferrets water in heavy water dishes, but the ferrets usually end up playing in the water, digging all of the water out, making a soggy mess, or spilling food and/or litter into the dish. This not only makes a big mess, but also fouls the water and makes it undrinkable. The water bottle method is more sanitary and easier to maintain. In warmer months, it's a good idea to keep some water in a bowl for your ferret to use in case he becomes too warm. Skinny-dipping is a real treat for most ferrets, especially during hot weather.

The Litter Box

Anything that eats and drinks is also going to need a place to go to the bathroom. In the case of a ferret, that place is a litter box. Look for a pan with sides at least 3 inches high all the way around. If the sides are any lower, you'll likely have litter (and waste) all over the floor. Small cat litter boxes work fine, so do small plastic boxes.

Corners are good places for litter boxes.

Litter boxes with sides at least three inches high help contain litter and waste.

The litter box will need to be secured in the cage, or your ferret will likely tip it over as he tries to burrow beneath it. Binder clips and bungee cords both work well. Whatever method you use, you will want something that you can easily remove, but that the ferret won't be tempted to play with.

Purchase a few litter boxes to strategically place around your home in areas that your ferret is likely to go. Most ferrets do not like to travel far to find a litter box. In fact, very few will do so. Even a well-trained ferret can be so intent on playing that he doesn't recognize nature's call until he doesn't have time to make it very far to find a pan. And to a ferret that needs to "go," any corner looks like a litter box.

Litter-ally Speaking

Because ferrets like to play in their litter, most regular cat litters are not good for ferrets. Clay litters are very dusty and can cause respiratory problems in ferrets. Clumping clay litters have been known to clump up inside breathing passages and cause respiratory arrest. Wood shavings are not a good idea for ferrets either; in addition to being dusty, they may contain aromatic oils that can cause respiratory problems in ferrets. Never use any kind of cedar chips or shavings with ferrets. They contain harmful phenols that are unhealthy for ferrets and other small mammals. Wood pellets are excellent for ferret litter. There are also some recycled newspaper pellets on the market that have worked well for many ferret owners. They are not only good for the environment, but they are just as clean as the wood pellets and are safer than clay litters.

Bedding

You will need something soft for your ferret to cuddle

up in. Old towels, blankets, sheets, or soft clothing such as jeans or sweatshirts work great. You will also need a hammock. Old T-shirts make great hammocks. Weave the arms through the top of the cage and use binder clips to hold up the two bottom ends. Ferrets are creatures of comfort, and they like soft, cuddly items. Bedding and hammocks made from sheepskin or synthetic sheepskin will be special favorites for them. Be sure to wash all bedding on a regular basis. Much of the odor associated with ferrets is actually on their bedding rather than on the ferret.

Ferret-Proofing Your Home

Before you let your new ferret run loose around your house, you will need to ferret-proof your home. A ferret is a small, curious creature and can easily find his way into places you never thought he could go. If the ferret finds that his head will fit through an opening, the body will soon follow.

Ferrets can end up in or on strange places.

Household Hazards

Although it sounds strange, you will need to crawl around on your hands and knees looking for small holes, crevices, loose ventilation covers, etc. that your ferret could crawl through. Even if your ferret will be confined to certain rooms, sooner or later, he will slip past the barriers and get into an "off-limits" area. It is better to be prepared for this event in advance so you don't have to panic wondering if the ferret is trapped somewhere, or worse yet, loose outdoors.

Toys

Be careful when you are choosing toys for your ferrets. Soft rubber and latex toys should be avoided because your ferret can chew off pieces and end up with life-threatening intestinal blockages. Ideal toys include: plastic balls with bells, plastic golf balls, squeaky stuffed animals (made for dogs or very small children), dryer, drain pipe, or cardboard tubing, and any home-made toys you can make by recycling household items. Ferrets are also just as happy with cardboard boxes, plastic grocery bags, and the wrapper their toy came in.

Ferrets like variety and they get bored easily. Alternate any toys you give them so they always have something "new" to play with. If they haven't seen a toy in several days, they'll react as if they've never seen it before.

You will need to check all appliances for holes and areas that a ferret could get inside(especially refrigerators, since some of them are designed so that a ferret could get up inside the back and become injured on the fan). Dryers should be double-checked, as they have tubing that will look very intriguing to a ferret, and that tubing leads to the great outdoors through the exit vent. (Some savvy ferret owners place a cage of sorts around the exit vent, just in case their sneaky ferret makes it that far.) Kitchen cabinets occasionally have open spaces in the back that can lead into the walls or to open basements or crawl spaces. A recliner or pullout sofa bed is a death trap for a ferret that gets up in the gears and springs. When the owner goes to recline or to pull out the sofa bed, the ferret can be seriously hurt or killed.

Make sure that your ferrets are in their cage or safely ensconced in a different area of the house before anyone is allowed to sit in, or lean back in a recliner. Even a couch can be very dangerous to ferrets. Most furniture has a thin fabric lining that a ferret can easily get through, and then crawl up inside the couch and into the springs. If someone happens to sit on the furniture while the ferret is in the springs, it can be disastrous. To prevent this, you can either staple hardware cloth over the bottom of the couch or nail a piece of plywood that's been cut to fit over it. Depending on the design of your furniture, you might consider taking off the sofa legs and letting the furniture sit flat on the floor, so that the ferret cannot crawl underneath it.

Box-spring furniture poses special dangers to ferrets

Is Your Home Ferret-Proof?

Never underestimate the ability of a ferret to be able to get into trouble in a place that you thought was safe for him. Ferrets are able to "weasel" through the smallest of openings, and are able to move extremely heavy objects out of their way if they think there is something interesting just beyond their reach. Ferret-proofing is not something that is done once and then forgotten about. It is a constant endeavor to stay one step ahead of these furry bandits. The following are some of the main areas of concern when ferret proofing your home.

Kitchen and bathroom cabinets–There is usually a gap that

your ferret could easily get into and there could be an opening into the wall of which you were not aware.

Window and door screens–Always make sure that there are no tears in them and they are securely fitted. Keep in mind that ferrets can very easily tear through most screens, so it is definitely wise to keep your windows and doors closed while the ferrets are out and about.

Appliances–Check under or behind the refrigerator, oven, washer, dishwasher, etc. to be sure that there is no way for a ferret to get inside the appliance even when it is closed. Before running any dishwasher, washing machine, or clothes dryer, always check inside and make sure that no ferret made his way in when you weren't looking.

Beds, couches, and recliners–A box spring, couch, or any other furniture that has springs is an accident waiting to happen for a ferret. An easy way to combat this problem is to staple a sheet pulled tight, a plastic carpet protector, or a piece of plywood to the bottom of your furniture. Recliners and sofa beds are great to have, but if you're going to own a ferret it really has to go, be modified, or you (and everyone in your house) must be extremely careful! A ferret can get caught in the moving wires, clamps etc., without your realizing it.

Electric wires, computer wires, and phone cords– Some ferrets are prone to chew on wires, which can have disastrous and sometimes deadly results. To help avoid this situation, you can pull all the wires together and through a plastic wire protector (or other tubing). If that fails, or if it is impossible to do for some reason, be sure you have pulled the wires up out of eye view of the ferret, and supervise him when he is in a room with unprotected wiring.

Open railings–If you live in a multi-level home and your ferrets are allowed full access, open stair or balcony railings can present a big hazard to your ferret, who may decide that he is related to a flying squirrel and may take a flying leap into the wild blue yonder. You can either restrict your ferret to the lower level of your home by using a gate or other blocking device, or you can purchase hardware cloth to intertwine between the spindles to protect your ferret from falling through.

Poisons–A lot of items that might not be poisonous to humans can have a deadly effect on ferrets. Something as seemingly innocent as a bowl of potpourri or a cigarette butt in an ashtray can mean death to an inquisitive ferret. Be sure that all cleaning chemicals are behind a locked (and well sealed) door, and that all potentially harmful houseplants are out of your ferret's reach.

Choking Hazards–Some common household items that you might not consider potentially dangerous to your ferret include the buttons on your remote control, toys that can splinter into pieces if chewed, packing peanuts, pencil erasers, earrings, children's plastic building blocks, bread ties, pen caps, and anything small enough for a ferret to swallow. Intestinal blockages are extremely common with ferrets, as they will put anything in their mouths that appears interesting.

Gates

It can sometimes be impossible to completely ferret-proof your entire home, even with the best of intentions. In these cases, you will want to block off rooms that are dangerous. An easy way to make a removable door block is to take an average wood-frame baby gate, buy vinyl or linoleum, cut it to fit, and staple it onto both parts of the baby gate. This way, the gate is still adjustable, but the ferret cannot crawl up it or get through it. Other options are to cut a piece of plywood or plastic to fit, put it in brackets, and just slide it in and out as needed.

Holidays can be a stressful time for ferrets.

'Tis the Season (to be Careful!)

When the holiday season arrives, it's easy to forget that our celebrations can prove stressful, or even dangerous, to our pets. The very fact that our lives become so busy during this time of year can be stressful to our pets, who are used to having our undivided attention. Suddenly, they are not only seeing less of their people, but they're also experiencing strange sounds and sights throughout their previously safe haven.

If your ferret roams free in the home at any time, his attraction to glitzy holiday decor can create a major health hazard. Most ferrets will happily chew on electrical cords, which will likely be more accessible with Christmas trees and holiday lights in the home. Make sure that all electrical cords are tacked up out of reach, or get some flexible plastic hose or tubing to encase the wires.

Inquisitive ferrets may chew on or swallow ornaments and decorations, which could potentially cause an intestinal blockage or choking, so close supervision or confinement away from decorations will likely be necessary.

Foil tinsel, ribbon, and other string-like items are irresistible to some ferrets as playthings but if they are ingested, they can also cause serious intestinal blockages. Candles may be attractive to your pet as well, so make sure they are not accessible. Candles are a double danger for ferrets–they cause burns as well as blockages if they're eaten. Even something as innocent as "spray-on" snow can prove to be mildly toxic to our pets.

Ferrets as Presents

Although you may think that everyone should have a ferret, remember that it is not a good idea to give pets as presents. With all the excitement of the holiday season, a new pet may have a hard time settling in, and it is more difficult for new owners to get into a routine of caring for the pet. If someone on your gift list really wants a ferret, wrap up some ferret toys and other supplies with a gift certificate or a note from a pet store or breeder promising a ferret from you once the holidays are over.

Holiday plants are beautiful, but they can be dangerous. Poinsettias are not highly toxic but do have a substance in the leaves that is very irritating to the skin, as well as to the lining of the stomach and intestines. Mistletoe is toxic (especially the berries), and should always be kept out of the reach of pets (and children). Holly berries are also very toxic, and the needles of Christmas trees (pines, cedars, and firs) can also cause irritation and problems if ingested.

Not only can the holiday décor be dangerous to your ferrets, but the special foods that we serve and eat during the holidays can create problems. Be sure that there are no packages under your tree containing chocolate goodies, as chocolate contains theobromine, which can be quite toxic to smaller animals, even at fairly low doses. Other holiday treats may not be quite so dangerous but can still create problems if they're eaten, especially in excess. Keep your ferret on his regular diet and don't be tempted to let him partake in holiday sweets and other goodies.

Be sure to keep your ferret safely locked in his cage during holiday parties. Not only is the ferret more likely to be accidentally injured in a crush of holiday revelers, but he is also more likely to get into trouble with his ferret hijinks when his people are busy entertaining guests. It's a good idea to place your ferret behind a locked door to keep a well-meaning

Beware of Holiday Dangers

Although the holidays are happy occasions, they can be a dangerous time for ferrets. Be wary of the following during the holiday season.

Alcoholic beverages—Just a few drops of liquor can cause alcohol poisoning or coma for a ferret.

Artificial snow—This is possibly poisonous, can cause digestive upset, and can be a respiratory irritant if inhaled.

Candles—Flames or dripping wax can burn your pet or singe his whiskers or hair.

Electrical cords—Ferrets can be shocked, burned, or electrocuted by chewing on exposed electrical cords. .

Decorations—Shiny decorations, while bringing a festive atmosphere to your home, can be dangerous to your ferret. Glass ornaments, garland, and tinsel, can be choking hazards. Decorate with the ferret in mind, or keep him in a safe place during the entire holiday season.

Fireplaces—Keep a fire screen in front of a fireplace while in use.

Food—Keep your ferret on a strict diet during the holidays. Don't be tempted to let him enjoy your holiday goodies, such as cookies and candy.

Decorative lights—Ferrets can become tangled in the strands of lights and this can lead to burns from the hot bulbs. They can create the same hazards as electric cords.

Holiday plants—Holly, ivy, mistletoe, and poinsettias are all poisonous to ferrets.

Gift-wrapping—Ribbon, trim, polystyrene foam packaging, wrapping foil, and wrapping paper are dangerous if eaten by your pet. Check all wrapping paper and boxes before putting them outside in the trash to be sure your ferret isn't hiding inside.

Christmas trees—Your ferret will more than likely try to climb the Christmas tree. To prevent the tree from falling over, place a hook in the ceiling and tie nylon yarn to the top of the tree, and then secure this to the ceiling. Don't allow your ferret to drink from the Christmas tree stand.

guest from inadvertently allowing him out of his cage and to possibly get hurt or lost if he darts out a door left open by a departing guest.

Try to minimize changes in your ferret's normal routine during the holidays by placing his cage in a quieter part of the home if there are a lot of visitors around. If you will be traveling, make sure you bring familiar belongings or toys along for your pet.

Okay, you've ferret-proofed your home, purchased a place for him to live, and found toys and bedding that will make him happy and comfortable. All systems are go–it's time to bring home the new addition!

Final Holiday Tips

Keep to your routine with your ferret as much as possible. If you spend time with him at the same time every day, try to continue doing so. If you feed, clean, or let him run free at the same time every day, do so as often as possible. This will help keep your pet's world consistent, and he'll deal with other holiday stresses much easier.

Make certain that you have the full details of how to contact your vet or the acting emergency vet during the holidays. A little foresight might help your pet survive a holiday accident.

The Adjustment Period

Once you've purchased your new ferret and brought him home, you may think that the hard times are over and only the fun times are ahead. Sometimes, however, there will be a period of adjustment for both you and your ferret before you can get to enjoy one another's company.

Although you should certainly spend as much time as possible with your new pet, it's not a good idea to force him into anything he doesn't feel comfortable doing for a few days. If he doesn't seem sure of himself being allowed full run of a room (or the entire house), let him stay in his cage until he is more confident with his surroundings. Sit by his cage and read the newspaper aloud,

Ferrets need time to adjust to a new home.

Teach children to respect the new family pet.

and sing or talk to him so he becomes familiar with the sound of your voice (and those of your family members). Make sure he has lots of interesting toys, the same food he was eating at his previous home, and a little bit of the bedding from his previous home as well.

Children and Ferrets

If you have children, make sure that they understand the rules before they are allowed to interact with the new ferret. Remember that unless the ferret was raised in a home with children, he is likely going to be a little overwhelmed by the rapid movements and louder voice of a child. Be certain that your children understand this, and act accordingly.

The children should obey the following rules:

• Treat the ferret as they should treat all pets, with respect, love, and kindness.

• Don't pick up the ferret unless an adult supervises them. Although ferrets are quite hardy, being dropped can easily break limbs or cause other injuries.

• Leave the ferret alone while he is sleeping. Just as you or I are a little grumpy when awakened from a sound sleep, the ferret will be, too. There will be plenty of "awake time" to share together later.

• Don't be upset if the ferret steals his or her toys. To a ferret, any brightly colored item within his grasp is fair game.

• Never taunt or torment the ferret. This will cause aggression, and it's not acceptable behavior for children to display when dealing with any pet or a person.

Help maintain the rules that you've set down for acceptable ferret behavior. Don't allow the children to play rough with the ferret if you are not allowing the ferret to nip or bite.

To a ferret, rough play is going to involve teeth and nails. If you play rough with a ferret, be prepared to break out the first aid kit! Take responsibility for your own actions. The ferret should not be punished for playing what appears to him to be normal ferret games. A ferret can't be blamed for not always realizing that human skin is more tender than their ferret playmates' skin.

Hopefully, your children and their friends will be enthralled by the new ferret and will want to hold him and play with him, but give your ferret some quiet time to adjust to his new home before he has too many visitors. Extra excitement, noise, and too much handling by strangers can stress out the ferret and make him nervous. Keep visitors to a minimum for the first few days until the ferret has settled into his surroundings.

Patience

Be patient if your ferret acts nervous or afraid. If you've adopted a young ferret, remember that this little guy has been through quite a lot for such a youngster. He was pulled away from mother and littermates at an early age, anesthetized for major surgery, and, probably before he was fully recuperated, packed into a shipping crate with a bunch of other ferrets and shipped in a noisy truck or in the belly of an airplane to go to yet another strange situation. If he came from a pet store, he was likely tossed in with a passel of other new ferrets and gawked at by hundreds of noisy humans every day–until you came along and plucked him from his cage and brought him into yet another strange situation. You can't really blame him for being just a little overwhelmed, now can you?

Noise

Most ferrets don't make much noise. This doesn't necessarily mean that they're unhappy, just that you're lucky enough to have chosen a quiet one. Just like people, some ferrets are more vocal than others. While one ferret may race dizzily around the room clucking in an excited frenzy, his cagemate may be racing around with equal energy, but without making a sound. Both are exhibiting behavior that is normal for them as individuals.

Part 2

Sing or talk to your pet. Soon he'll know your voice.

Ferrets benefit from "quiet time."

Helping Your Ferret Adjust to his New Home

Adjusting to life in a new location is going to be stressful on your ferret, no matter how careful and thoughtful you are. Here are a few ways that you can make things easier for him.

√ Leave him in his cage until he realizes that it is his new home and that it is a safe haven for him.

√ Be sure that everyone in the family and any visitors (which should be kept at a minimum for the first few days) understand the need to be quiet and make no sudden movements near the ferret's cage.

√ Keep other pets locked out of the room where the ferret is being kept. Be sure to spend time with them and give them treats so they don't become jealous.

√ Let the ferret make the decision as to when it's time to socialize. If he wants to stay hidden in a snuggle sack or in a box you've provided for that reason, let him.

√ Once your ferret decides that he wants to meet everyone, make sure that all family members are given a quick lesson in how to pick him up and hold him.

√ Have treats available for all family members to give him so he knows he is among friends.

√ Continue keeping the noise and activity very low key, especially when the ferret is out of his cage and in unfamiliar territory.

Let your pet decide when he wants to socialize with his new family.

√ If possible, keep a radio playing soft soothing music to provide a comforting background noise for your ferret.

If you've taken in an older or "rescued" ferret, be aware that he will still need time to adjust to his new home. Everything looks new and different to him. His surroundings smell strange, and he doesn't know any of his new family members yet.

As the ferret's new owner, it's up to you to make this new place feel like home to him. Keep things as calm as possible around him, keep loud noises to a minimum, and consider playing soft music when you aren't in the room with the ferret, so he doesn't feel lonely.

Your new ferret may be a little timid for a while, but within a few days he should be scampering around the room, making his little chuckling sounds, getting into mischief, and making you laugh at his antics.

Handling Your Ferret

Want a ferret that loves to be held and petted? It's the nature of most ferrets to want to wriggle and play when they're picked up. However, if you start out from the beginning being in charge when you pick them up, you can quickly change their mind. Once you pick your ferret up, keep holding him on your terms. No matter how much he may want down, no matter how much he squirms and wriggles, keep holding him until you are ready to put him down. Once he settles down (usually with a big sigh of resignation), give him a tasty treat. He will quickly get the idea that being held has its rewards. Soon, you will have a ferret that loves to be held and cuddled.

Don't Get Too Close

It is never a good idea to put your face close to a ferret's face or feet. However gentle the ferret may be, he can inflict quite a bit of damage in a short time, while perhaps only meaning to play. Children should be taught to never hold a ferret near their face.

Part 2

Tasty, healthy treats help convince your pet that being held has its rewards.

Scruffing Your Ferret

Scruffing is a safe and painless way of holding your ferret and getting him to remain still. Knowing the proper way to scruff a ferret can make many situations (such as giving your ferret medicine, correcting bad behavior, and trimming his toenails) much easier not only for you, but also for your ferret.

Scruffing gives you a lot more control over your ferret than the usual way you hold him. Simply grab the loose skin behind the ferret's neck and pick him up. This should cause him to remain still. Support his bottom with your other hand so you don't hurt his back. Most ferrets will open their mouths and yawn when they're scuffed, but even if the ferret tries to nip at you, your hands are safe from his teeth and nails in this position.

You can scruff your ferret by picking him up by the fur on the back of his neck.

To ensure that your ferret becomes tame and affectionate with humans, it is important that you handle him frequently and correctly from the day he joins your family. Picking up a ferret incorrectly or infrequently could lead to your ferret being permanently frightened and may cause him to become aggressive.

Remember that most small animals in the wild are prey. Therefore, it stands to reason that if an animal is approached from above, he will see a large shadow or feel hands coming out of nowhere to pick him up. This will cause the animal to become scared. Before you pick up your ferret, be sure that he always sees or hears you. Don't startle him, or he might accidentally bite you while "defending" himself. Your ferret will indicate when he wants to be picked up by holding onto your leg or by grabbing your wrist when you extend your hand.

Ferrets should be picked up from behind using two hands, one hand supporting the chest and shoulder area, and the other hand cradling the hips and rear legs. Gently lift the ferret and hold him against your chest. A ferret should never be grabbed at or be picked up by the tail. Be sure that all children and visitors are taught the correct way to pick up and hold your ferret before they are allowed to play with him.

Before you pick up your ferret while he's in his cage, make sure that he is awake and alert. Let him decide when he is ready to come to you. Talk to him, as your voice will make him aware that you are near him. Using the same words and offering a treat until he becomes used to handling will go a long way toward making him enjoy "cuddle time."

Ferret Introductions

If you are introducing a new ferret into your household and you already have a ferret, you should quarantine the new ferret for several days to make sure that he doesn't show any signs of illness. After the quarantine period, put your new ferret's cage right up next to your current ferret's cage. This will allow them to get used to one another. Take some of the bedding from the new ferret's cage and place it in your current ferret's cage (and vice versa). This will help the ferrets get used to one another's scent.

Let the new ferret and your current ferret interact only under your direct supervision until you are satisfied that they have become friends. Don't be surprised if they start to wrestle. Wrestling helps establish each ferret's place in the group order. One ferret will usually bite the other ferret by the scruff of the neck and try to drag him across the floor (with much tumbling and twisting). This is usually done with a lot of vocalizing and hissing. Don't separate the ferrets while they are wrestling unless they are drawing blood or one ferret seems too stressed out. Hopefully, things will balance out as they get used to one another, and they will start playing for longer periods of time without any wrestling incidents.

Pick up your ferret from behind, with two hands.

Part 2

Quarantine a new ferret from others you may have already.

To help your current ferret bond with the new ferret, try putting a liquid vitamin supplement such as Linatone™ or Ferretone™ on the new ferret's head. Then, while holding both ferrets, let your ferret lick the Ferretone™ off of the new ferret's head. After a few minutes, put some Ferretone™ on the other ferret and let the new ferret lick it off. This helps them to get over their scent differences. Be sure to give both ferrets lots of special treats and attention, let them see that they are both special to you, and that you expect them to become friends.

Introducing Your Ferret to Other Pets

Most ferrets are so inquisitive that they will not only enjoy meeting new people, but other animals as well. While ferret owners sometimes fear that their ferret will either harm or be harmed by their other pets, if you handle their introduction correctly, the ferrets will likely become the best of friends and playmates.

Be aware that there are some species that will probably never be happy, safe, or content around your ferret. Because

Off to a Good Start

Because you may be offering treats to your new ferret as you work on making him happy in his new home, make sure that you don't start bad habits by feeding him inappropriate snacks. Snacks with too much sugar or not enough protein can do more harm than good. Nutritionally sensible treats that your ferret will love include meat-based treats or fatty acid supplements. Cooked chicken, chicken or turkey baby foods, chicken livers, cooked egg, or chicken or turkey-flavored cat or ferret treats will definitely tickle your ferret's fancy. A few raisins a day likely won't cause any problems, but they have no nutritional value for a ferret, and they do contain sugar. Avoid giving the ferret fresh fruits or raw vegetables. Large amounts of raw vegetables and fruits can cause intestinal blockages in ferrets, as they cannot digest vegetable matter.

of their genetics, a ferret will always see members of the rodent family as prey. (Smaller birds will likely not be safe around a rodent for that same reason.) Trying to introduce the two species could have disastrous, if not fatal, results.

By that same token, be careful when introducing your ferret to a breed of dog that was bred to hunt smaller animals. Sometimes hunting breeds and hounds have a tougher time thinking of a ferret as a playmate instead of a plaything or prey. Although most breeds of dog may quickly adapt to the new member of the family, most cats like to take their time.

When introducing your other pets to the ferret (and vice versa), it is of ultra importance that you strictly supervise the initial meeting. It's a good idea to have your dog on a leash, or your cat held firmly until you can gauge her reactions to this new musky-smelling interloper to their territory. Don't use food or treats when introducing the two species, as jealousy over food can create an aggressive situation. Pay just as much attention to the established pet as you are paying to the ferret to avoid any protective jealousy patterns.

No matter how well your pets seem to get along, they should never be allowed to play together unsupervised. The most well meaning dog can easily get so involved with a game of chase or wrestle that he might accidentally wound or kill his ferret friend.

Fun Ways to Bond

Get to know your ferret by playing simple games with him. One bonding experience you can have with your new ferret is to place a treat beneath an overturned flowerpot and see how long it takes him to discover the treat, and how to get to it.

Toss a towel over the ferret's head and see how long it takes him to back out from beneath it. Then, drag the towel away and give your ferret something new and fun to chase. Most ferrets will eventually grab hold of the towel and hold on for dear life as they are dragged around the floor. Your ferret will enjoy spending quality time with you and learn to trust you as he plays.

Newly introduced ferrets may wrestle for dominance.

Part 2

Do's and Don'ts for Introducing Ferrets to Other Family Pets

Before you begin filling in your new ferret's social calendar, you should take time to assess his likes and dislikes. If he has already shown an avid dislike or fear of other animals, you'll have to work up his confidence a bit before introducing him into a new relationship for which he may not be ready. If, however, he is at the front of his cage trying to play with the dog's nose or with the cat's tail, there's a good chance that you could be witnessing the start of a beautiful relationship.

• Do restrain both animals until you're sure that they are well acquainted and neither is showing any aggressive tendencies toward the other. Be prepared to separate the two at the first hint of discontent on either's part.

• Don't expect a ferret to enjoy being pals with a rodent or a breed of dog that was originally bred to hunt small animals.

• Don't rush the introduction. Let the animals take their time. Never shove the two together or attempt to force them to interact.

• Don't neglect the old pet in favor of the new one.

• Don't bring food or other treats into the equation when introducing pets

Closely supervise meetings between family pets and the new ferret.

New Owner Misconceptions

Ferrets sometimes do things that make new owners think that their pet has a serious problem. Many vets have been called by frantic first-time ferret owners who were sure that the ferret had fallen into a coma. Actually, ferrets sometimes sleep so soundly that they seem to be dead. Even if you pick them up, thump their chest, shake them, and pinch their toes, they hang from your hand as limp as a rag. After naptime is over, the ferret will sleepily open his eyes and yawn as he wonders what is going on. Some ferrets do this so often that their owners get used to it. Others do it so seldom that it creates a panic each time because the ferret owner is afraid the pet is in a coma or has died. If the ferret is warm, has a moist pink mouth, and is breathing regularly but slowly, he is not dead, just sleeping soundly. Comatose ferrets usually drool, have cold extremities, and may stiffen and moan during convulsions.

Is my Ferret Cold?

Another mistake made by new owners is thinking that their new ferret is cold. Often when you wake your ferret up and take him out of his cage, he trembles. People new to the world of ferrets sometimes interpret this as fear or think that the ferret is shivering because the room is too cold. Adult ferrets tremble for many reasons such as excitement, anticipation, and probably other pleasurable ferret emotions that we humans can neither imagine nor begin to describe in words. They rarely shiver with cold, and fear is expressed differently. When your ferret has had a chance to run around for a few minutes and gets some of the excitement out of his system, you will notice that he is no longer trembling, even when you pick him up.

Most ferrets enjoy meeting new people.

Sleeping Snugly

Some owners of multiple ferrets get upset when their ferrets refuse to sleep in their own beds. Given a choice, ferrets like to sleep together for comfort, and in cold weather, for warmth. When given several hammocks or sleep sacks to sleep in, a group of ferrets will usually all get into one. This does not mean that there is anything wrong with the other beds. Another worry is that whoever gets in first ends up on the bottom of the pile and may not be able to breathe. Don't worry; even though the ferret appears to be at risk, there is no record of adult ferrets smothering another in their piles.

Ferret Madness?

When first released from their cages to play, many ferrets burst out of the door, run, leap, twist in the air, and carelessly collide with solid objects. They might run over to your feet, nip at your shoe, and go on another race around the house, sometimes making soft chuckling noises as they do. To the new ferret owner, it appears as if the ferret has gone

Natural Behaviors

As frustrating and unusual as you'll find some of your new ferret's behaviors, these are the very traits that early ferret owners found most attractive. The following is a list of common ferret behaviors and their original purposes. Keep in mind that very few other species have retained so much of their original traits throughout the centuries.

Biting: Necessary for killing prey (rodents).

Digging: Necessary to search and destroy prey.

Ability to "ferret" into almost any tight space: Same as above.

Cunning and sly behavior: Necessary to be a formidable adversary for savvy prey.

mad. Since this careening ferret will likely back up, arch his back, jump, and perhaps even hiss at the hand that reaches for him, the owner becomes convinced that the pet is either having a seizure of some sort, experiencing some sort of rage syndrome, or truly has gone completely crazy. Don't worry; none of these suppositions is true.

Ferrets do not try to avoid running into things, probably because their vision is poor and they like to move at high speed. This behavior is just a normal ferret, expressing normal ferret exuberant behavior at being let out to play, and is a good indicator that the ferret is feeling well. Ferrets have a very high threshold of pain and truly do not appear to notice bumps that would make most other animals stop and lick the spot that was hurt.

Dragging the Hindquarters

Another action that causes alarm in some new ferret owners is that after using the litter box, some ferrets drag their hindquarters along the floor, the way dogs do when they have impacted anal glands. Sometimes the ferret's owner will take the ferret to a veterinarian, worried that the ferret has a problem with the descenting surgery, or that he is itchy because of tapeworms or pinworms, constipated, or is losing control of his hind legs. In fact, your ferret is just using your floor for toilet paper. This is another very good reason for locating the litter box on a floor that can easily be washed. Although ferrets don't cover their stools in the litter box, they do try to maintain their body hygiene.

The settling-in period is the most important time in a ferret's life. How you handle it will ensure whether he is a neurotic and timid little fellow, or a captivating, precocious ferret. Be sure that your ferret doesn't get any unpleasant surprises during his first weeks with you, and he'll repay you with trust and affection for years to come.

Although he may spend a few days hiding in his bedding, soaking up the sights and sounds around him, before you know it, your ferret will be racing to the top of his cage to see you when you enter the room. Then you'll know that it's time to introduce him to more of the world around him. If you continue to keep things quiet and calm around the ferret, he will gain more confidence and become a happy, well-adjusted member of the family.

Part 2

Housing Your Ferret

Although buying a cage and housing your ferret was briefly discussed previously, we will discuss in depth everything that you need to know to give your ferret friend a happy home.

A Free-Roaming Ferret?

Some ferret owners prefer not to cage their ferrets at all and let them roam freely around the house. While this certainly is wonderful for the ferret, this type of ferret lifestyle certainly carries many more responsibilities for the owner. Constant and responsible ferret-proofing is a must. To be completely safe, some areas of the house, such as closets, kitchens, laundry rooms, and bathrooms, should remain inaccessible to ferrets.

Be prepared to keep your ferret safe and happy at home.

Keep some areas off limits to your ferret.

Play it Safe

It's a very good idea that your ferrets be caged when no one is home. In case of a fire or other emergency, ferrets that are outside their cage will be much more difficult (if not impossible) to locate and rescue if necessary. Do all you can to keep your ferret safe and happy.

A bell on a safety collar will help you find your free-roaming pet.

Free-range ferrets are more difficult to toilet train, and almost every corner in the house may have to be lined with newspaper or have its own litter box. Every ferret in the home should have a belled safety collar on when he's out of his cage, so he can be found even when he might not really want to be. Owners of free-range ferrets still need to have cages set up and available to use for time-outs, for when company is over, or for isolating an ill ferret.

Whether you plan for your ferret to be caged or free-roaming, you need to have a nicely- sized cage ready for him when he arrives at your home. This is important for many reasons, not the least of which is that it makes litter training much easier on everyone. The ferret will feel safer in a strange place if he is confined to a small area that will quickly become familiar to him. Bringing a ferret into a strange situation and turning him loose with full run of your home is like setting you down in the middle of a bustling airport in a strange city of giants where you don't speak the language. This situation can be very frightening, especially for a baby ferret that has already been through quite a bit in such a short lifetime.

The Cage

A strong, metal mesh cage is usually the best choice for a ferret's cage. Most cages are made of galvanized metal wire, but powder-coated wire (like an enamel) is preferred for longevity, ease of cleaning, and the smooth surface. Wire cages may have sharp edges, however, which may need to be filed down or protected by a wire guard. The wire openings on a cage must be no larger than 1 x 2 inches, or the ferret may be able to escape. While you may see some pet stores keeping ferrets in aquarium-like enclosures, they are not recommended as full-time cages. They do not provide enough room or ventilation, and they can trap heat and humidity.

Learn from Experience

Having a ferret loose in the house all the time is really not recommended for a first-time ferret owner who may need more experience in understanding ferret behaviors and ferret-proofing issues. After you've lived with a ferret for just a short while, you'll realize how crafty they are and realize that what you thought was securely "ferret-proofed" may not be so "proof" at all!

A Cage is a Must

No matter how much you might want your ferret to be loose in your home, there will always be periods of time when he will need to be in his cage for safety's sake, such as if you have company, when you're vacuuming, or cleaning with strong chemicals. A temporary cage will allow your ferret somewhere safe to stay while you go about your daily routine.

Running free in a new home may scare a baby ferret

Part 2

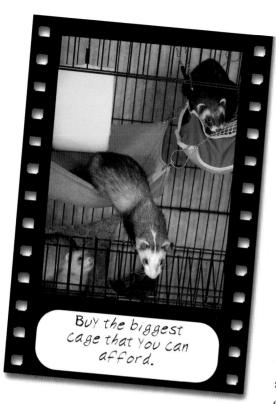

Buy the biggest cage that you can afford.

If you plan to keep your ferret caged when you're not home, and you'll be gone most of the day, the cage should be about 2 feet x 3 feet x 2 feet high. If necessary, a second ferret could share that size cage. Of course, a nice, big "condo" with lots of levels and hammocks (placed judiciously to prevent falls from the top shelf) is better. If you find that your ferret uses the trays on some of the shelves as a bathroom, try putting a small plastic shoebox on that level as a "backup" litter box. If that doesn't work, just make sure that every level is covered with soft bedding.

Where to Get a Cage

You can make the ferret's cage yourself if you are handy with a saw and screwdriver. Your handmade version may be cheaper than a store-bought cage, and you can get exactly the size and configuration that you want. Be sure that if you make your own cage, you sand down the cage and do not leave any rough edges or sharp objects exposed.

Almost all major pet stores and pet-supply catalogs have lots of cages you can buy. Multiple-level "cat condo" type cages are probably the most popular store-bought cages. Some super stores now carry ferret cages, and there are usually some available through online auctions or through websites devoted to ferret merchandise. Make sure that you get a cage that is well made, with no sharp edges that can cut your ferret. There should be at least one door that is large enough to take out the litter box for cleaning. The cage should come apart easily for the in-depth cleaning it will need.

When it comes to cages, bigger is better. Buy the biggest cage that you can afford. Your ferret is relying on you to keep his home a happy and safe place.

What Goes in the Cage?

You should incorporate some sort of "bedroom" in the cage for your ferret. A ferret won't be very happy sleeping on the open floor of a cage, even if he's on (or, more likely, under) a towel or shirt. Any small cardboard box or basket will work well as a bedroom. Old T-shirts and sweatshirts make excellent bedding for these beds, as long as they aren't too easily chewed to bits. Old towels usually work well too, though some ferrets tend to get their nails caught in the fibers.

If you decide that you still want to use some sort of bedding other than fuzzy or woven materials, you'll find that corn-cob bedding is just as convenient as using shavings and sawdust, is dust-free and somewhat safer (although there have been reports of ferrets ingesting the pellets which caused blockages) than the other options.

Other than food, water, a litter pan, bedding, and a bedroom, what you put in your ferret's cage

A small basket can suffice as a bedroom in your pet's cage.

Cage Accessories Checklist

To make your ferret's home a happy place, be sure to add the following accessories to the cage.

√ Two or more high-backed corner litter pans for ferrets (one or two for the cage and more for outside the cage).

√ Heavy ceramic food and water dishes or dishes that attach to the cage (use plastic ties to attach them if they're easily detachable).

√ A hanging water bottle.

√ Towels, old shirts, pieces of fabric, or a throw rug to line the bottom and levels of the cage (especially around the litter pan).

√ Hammocks, sleeping sacks, or soft sleeping tubes (make sure they are washable).

√ Toys, such as play tubes and tunnels (a must-have because ferrets love tunnels), hanging toys, rolling balls etc. (Buy toys that are dishwasher or washing machine safe to make cleaning easier.)

√ Recycled paper or wood pellet litter for ferrets.

Old sweatshirts make excellent bedding for ferrets.

Batten Down the Hatches

Be sure that the ferret's cage door fastens securely. You may even want to add a small lock or clip, as most ferrets can be very determined escape artists. Twist ties, cable ties, bungee cords, or bits of wire often work well for fastening down litter pans and food or water bowls so they don't become toys or missiles.

is largely up to you, because you know your ferret's likes and dislikes. Enough room to stretch and climb around is important, and different levels, ramps, and tunnels made from dryer hose or black drainage pipe will be greatly appreciated. Hammocks made from old jeans or shirts and a set of metal eyelets are very popular for both napping and playing.

All Packed and Ready to Go

Not only do you need to purchase a cage for your ferret while he is home, but you should also purchase a travel cage for him for fun travel and for veterinary and emergency trips. Travel cages (such as the The Nylabone® Fold-Away Pet Carrier) also work well as a place to give a "time-out" to a rambunctious ferret, or they can be used to isolate an ill ferret. You can also use them for a "bedroom" inside a larger cage, or as a place for the ferret that is loose in a larger area to sleep.

Most pet carriers are approved for airline travel, but if you plan to fly with your ferret, make sure that the carrier you have is suitable. Only one size of pet carrier is approved for under-the-seat air transportation, and the rest must travel in cargo.

If your ferret will be inside the carrier for any great length of time, it will be necessary to include a small litterpan. Plastic shoeboxes are a good size for this and can be fastened to the carrier floor with heavy-duty double-stick tape. Instead of litter, consider using baby or adult diapers to line the litter box or the entire carrier floor.

Cage Safety

When the ferret is loose, you may find that he likes to scale his condo cage from the outside, and sort of looks like a little fuzzy Superhero scaling a tall building. When he gets to the top, he'll take great pride in being able to push off all the things that accumulate up there—extra newspapers, treats, food, medicines, spare water bottles, bowls, and toys. It's a good idea to put a newspaper, a towel or a piece of wood on the top of the cage to keep the ferret from possibly getting his foot through the wires and then damaging his leg.

Cage Placement

Placement of the cage is as important as the choice of cage. While you want the ferret to feel like part of the family, you should be careful to not place him in such a busy location that he'll seldom get a quiet moment to rest. An office, den, or other secondary room that gets frequent, but not constant traffic is a good choice.

If you are thinking about putting the ferret's cage in the basement or garage, you should perhaps rethink the entire matter of getting a ferret. Ferrets are social creatures, and being banished to an area of your home that receives little attention other than quick walk-throughs will not give him enough interaction with humans. In addition, garages and basements are often too cold and drafty and may contain hazardous fumes. As a rule of thumb, your ferret should be kept in an area that you wouldn't mind living in.

Once you've decided what room of the house will best suit both you and the ferret, you must be sure that the cage isn't too near a heating or cooling source (such as a fireplace, heat duct, air-conditioning vent, etc.) or in a direct draft from a door that opens to the outdoors or other area that is not climate controlled. Placing the cage near a window might seem like a good idea, but during the summer months the direct sunlight could prove very uncomfortable to your furry

Your pet's cage can include rolling toys like this ball.

Lots of Toys

No ferret will be happy in a cage that has nothing but bare essentials such as food, water, and bedding. Ferrets must have interesting, thought-provoking toys. Some ideas for ferret toys that are as safe as they are fun include the following:

• Sturdy plastic toys (look in the cat and dog section of the pet store).

• Tennis balls and hard plastic balls.

• Balls with bells or other noisemakers inside.

• Cardboard boxes and paper bags.

• PVC pipes or commercial ferret tubes. (Lean them against different levels in a condo cage for some slip-sliding fun!)

• Hanging parrot toys (usually made with wood, heavy ropes, or bells).

• Rattles, teething rings, and other hard plastic toys made for human babies.

• Small stuffed toys with squeakers or other noisemakers inside. Be wary of toys with eyes and noses that can be chewed off and swallowed.

• Soft cloth bags for hiding and sleeping in. Some come with a layer of crinkly material inside that makes them extra interesting to ferrets.

• Play tents or houses.

Cage mates can share a ground-level playhouse.

friend. Be sure that the room is either climate controlled, or that you have taken pains to keep your ferret as comfortable as possible.

Keep it Cool

Remember that no matter where your ferret is (in his cage, playing in your home, or traveling in your car), it's important to keep in mind that ferrets don't handle changes in temperature the way people do. Because ferrets originally lived in a cooler climate and made their homes in underground burrows that were protected from the heat of summer's sun, they do not tolerate heat as well as animals that evolved in a warmer climate. Your ferret will let you know when he is too warm by panting or by displaying a grumpy behavior.

Cool Dudes!

If you aren't going to be around all day to spritz your ferret with water, you can place a damp towel over the top of the cage and place a bucket of water on top of that towel. Take another damp towel and place one end of it in the bottom of the bucket and the other end on the cage towel. The bucket towel will act as a wick to draw the water from the bucket, keeping the towel covering the cage wet. In that situation, having a fan blowing on the cage will help with the evaporation of the water in the towel, and thus aid the cooling process.

You can also fill 2-liter soda bottles (or milk jugs) with water and freeze them. Once they're frozen, put them inside long socks, a shirt, or other material and place them in the bottom of the ferret's cage where he can snuggle against them to stay cool. Don't let a fan blow directly on the frozen bottle, as cold air sinks when it is undisturbed, and you don't want to blow the cool air away from your ferret.

My Bed is Tooooo Hot

Be sure that your ferret's cage isn't located close to a furnace grate, heat duct opening, or fireplace. You may not think of that if you place the cage during the summer months, and by the time you remember when the heater turns on at fall's first frost, your ferret could have become uncomfortably warm.

Older or medically debilitated ferrets are more susceptible to temperature changes than younger or middle-aged ferrets. Ferrets can survive prolonged periods of uncomfortable temperatures with no obvious signs of distress, but the strain to their system may manifest itself in illness later on. In the case of repeated heat stress, the immune system can be permanently compromised, making the ferret susceptible to illness and disease.

If your home is air-conditioned, it should be easy to keep your ferret comfortable on hot summer afternoons. If you live in a warm climate and don't have air-conditioning or are suffering unseasonably warm temperatures for your area, keep a close eye on the heat index (not just the thermometer), and, as the temperature rises, take measures to ensure that your ferrets are kept cool and comfy.

Cage Cleaning

Your ferret's cage should be cleaned on a regular basis, not only for odor control, but also to maintain your ferret's health. When you are cleaning the cage, you can either let your

Ferrets love tunnels. Some have plastic tunnels in their cages.

The Cage and Other Pets

Your ferret's cage should be located in a room that can be closed away from noisy guests as well as from other pets. Even though your ferret is in a cage, a cat or dog can cause quite a bit of havoc if it attempts to break into your ferret's cage. Avoid stressing both pets by keeping them apart unless you're in the room, or until you are well satisfied that they are going to be friends.

ferret run loose, or you can put him inside his travel cage with a favorite toy or treat to keep him busy. It's a good idea to have an extra set of everything (bedding, dishes, and toys,) if possible, so no time is lost getting your ferret back into his cage.

The bedding and stuffed toys should be washed the same way that you wash your bathroom towels. Be sure that you rinse everything well and that the bedding and toys are thoroughly dry before you put them back inside the cage. Use fragrance free detergent to avoid eye or respiratory irritation in your ferret. Most people find that washing bedding once a week is sufficient.

The litter box should be scooped out daily and taken out and sterilized on a weekly basis. Food dishes should be washed daily if you are feeding your ferret anything other than dry kibble (the top level of the dishwasher works for most food and water bowls) and bi-weekly if you are feeding dry foods. Most plastic toys can also benefit from a trip through the dishwasher, as well.

Be sure you wash the bottom of the cage thoroughly, once everything has been removed,

Cleanups on the Go

For quick mini cleanups while traveling, keep a box of baby wipes near your ferret's pet carrier. These will clean up not only the ferret, but also the cage in case of an "accident."

Put Your pet in his Nylabone® Fold-Away Pet Carrier when cleaning his cage.

and be sure to scrub the ramps and upper levels. It's not a good idea to use carpet inside a ferret's cage, because it harbors odors that don't go away with vacuuming or other cleaning. Instead, use linoleum or vinyl that can be taken out and washed completely. Cutting two or three pieces of the same size will allow you to take the top layer out to be cleaned, but still leave another layer in place. When the piece you are cleaning is dry, place it on the bottom of the stack.

Although you want to be sure to get the cage clean, be careful not to use harsh cleaning chemicals that can be toxic if ingested by your ferret. Most pet owners have found that using antibacterial dish soap works well. Fill up the bathtub with hot soapy water to wash the cage parts and any other supplies that need a good cleaning. Drain the water from the tub and use the shower to rinse well.

Keeping your ferret's bedding, toys, litter box and cage clean will not only decrease the "ferret" odor, but also

Plastic toys can benefit from a trip through the dishwasher.

will deter fleas and will cut down on the possible transmission of bacterial and viral infections.

Once you've established that the place you've chosen for your ferret's cage is in a centrally located position, where he will see family members but not to excess, and he is not in a place that will be too hot or too cold or in a direct draft, it's time to put it in place and start adding supplies!

Part 2

Feeding and Nutrition

One of the first things you'll realize about your ferret is that the thing he loves the most in the world (other than you, of course) is food. The way to a ferret's heart is through his stomach. Since good nutrition is the most necessary requirement for maintaining a healthy ferret, providing your pet with the proper diet is of utmost importance.

Ferrets have very fast metabolisms and very short digestive systems, which makes their feeding requirements much more unique than the average pet's. While you'll find aisle after aisle of dog foods and cat foods in most pet stores, you'll be lucky to find one or two brands of specially formulated ferret kibble.

The way to a ferret's heart is through his stomach.

Ferrets look long, but they have short digestive tracts

Watch What You Feed Your Ferret

All foods, even foods that say they are intended solely for ferrets, are not created equally, so be careful what you are feeding your ferret. Some so-called "ferret foods" are simply repackaged (and price-increased) mink and cat foods. Learn to read labels and understand what you're reading

For many years, the common recommendation from vets and breeders was to feed ferrets a good-quality dry cat or kitten food. With the advent of more specialized research into the ferret's nutritional needs, most vets have changed their views and their recommendations considerably.

Although ferrets do have a somewhat similar dietary requirement to cats, their intestines are designed quite differently, so some important considerations must be made when choosing their diet. Since they lack the ability to derive much, if any, nutrition from plant matter, a ferret diet must be high in animal protein, relatively high in fat, and very low in fiber. Food passes through the digestive system of a ferret very quickly, so it must be formulated for easy digestion if it is to give the ferret any benefits at all.

How to Read Nutrition Labels

When you look at the nutrient analysis on a bag of ferret kibble, you will easily find the statement of the minimum levels of protein and fat in the diet. But that's not good enough. You also need to carefully examine the ingredient list and make sure that the ingredients back up the percentage claim in an acceptable manner. Since protein can come from a variety of sources (including plant matter that a ferret cannot digest), you need to make sure that the bulk of the protein is derived from meat and poultry products. You should

Learn to Read Ingredient Labels

To ensure that you are getting a food that is correctly formulated to give your ferret a long and healthy life, the ingredients should be listed as follows.

First listed: meats, or meat meal. Never meat by-products.

Always in the first three: fat

Never in the first three: fish

Never more than one of corn, soy, or wheat

Many pet foods, especially the inexpensive types, use corn as a major source of protein. For some species, this might be passably acceptable, but it will be indigestible and therefore useless to a ferret.

also make sure that the meat and poultry products are not listed as "meat by-products." Although it's true that these "by-products" may indeed be meat, most are no more digestible for ferrets than they would be for humans. Meat by-products include such things as chicken toenails, animal ligaments, bones, blood, and intestines. Some unscrupulous pet food manufacturers also include things such as ground-up rubber and other totally indigestible products that they can legally label as "protein." Learn to read your ingredient labels and know what you're buying for your pet.

The list of ingredients is based on their percentages in the food, from greatest to least, but the first ingredient listed isn't necessarily the one that makes up the bulk of the diet (for example, the first ingredient may only be 10 percent of the diet, with the rest of the ingredients combining to make up the remaining 90 percent).

Make sure your pet's diet is high in fat and protein and very low in fiber.

Ferrets eat frequently, usually every three to four hours.

Necessary Requirements

Ferrets need a diet that is a minimum of 34 to 36 percent protein and approximately 20 percent fat (and low fiber). Remember that you can't choose a food strictly by the numbers on the label. The source of the protein and other nutrients is more important than the quantity.

It's also important to do your homework about the manufacturer of the food you choose. Do they consistently use the same recipe? Do they change the recipe according to the price of the day for the various ingredients? Some manufacturers do not follow a strict regimen regarding their recipes.

Feeding Time

Ferrets also need to eat frequently, usually every three to four hours. The preferred feeding method is simply to have food available constantly. Feeding dry kibble is probably the most convenient and safest choice, as it can be left available at all times without concern for spoilage. Dry foods also have the added advantage of helping keep the teeth clean and tartar-free as well. Premium canned ferret (or cat) food can be given as a treat or supplement on occasion, but is not a good idea for a healthy ferret. An elderly or ill ferret should be fed whatever it takes to keep him in a good weight.

Almost all ferrets eat enough to meet their caloric needs.

Almost all ferrets will eat only enough to meet their caloric needs and will not become obese if allowed constant access to food. However, if you are having a problem with your ferret gaining too much weight, check with a vet to rule out a medical problem and ask for advice on how to meet the ferret's dietary needs while maintaining a good weight for his frame.

Ferret Foods

There are several packaged ferret diets now available and some are considered better than others. The best ones tend to be expensive, but if you find one with good quality, it will be worth the price. It's not a bargain if the animal has to eat twice as much of it to get the same amount of nutrition.

Snacks

Some suggestions for ferret treats include: cat treats, dry cereals, peanut butter on a bit of cracker, mashed banana, raisins, nuts, freeze-dried liver (sold as cat treats), and puffed rice cakes. You can pretty much feed your ferret anything that can be broken into small pieces. You never know what he is going to consider a special treat. If you find a treat that is good for him as well as tasty, be sure to keep some on hand in case your ferret gets sick and needs special tempting to get him to eat.

Part 2

Training Aids and Deterrents

Linatone™ or Ferretone™ are excellent vitamin supplement treats and work well as training aids. Be careful not to give your ferret too much, as these are high in fatty oils. A few drops a day are sufficient.

Deterrents, such as Bitter Apple™ or Bitter Lime™ can help keep a ferret away from cords or anything else he may want to chew on. Hot pepper sauce, alcohol, or grapefruit juice in a spray bottle may be used in extreme cases, too. Some ferrets develop a taste for Bitter Apple and this will actually encourage them to chew instead of deter them.

Consult your vet if your pet is gaining too much weight.

It's a good idea to change your ferret's food from time to time.

Unhealthy Foods?

We know that pesticides and other chemicals that are used in growing fruits and vegetables are not good for us, but consider how dangerous they can potentially be for our ferrets. Ferrets have digestive systems that are far more sensitive and smaller than our own, and some chemicals can cause hormone imbalances that can create or worsen existing behavioral problems. Buy organically grown foods whenever possible, and be sure you wash all fruits or vegetables before giving them to your ferret as a treat. Keep in mind, however, that ferrets do not digest fruits and vegetables easily, and they should only be given in small portions on occasion.

Although some foods are very high in protein from fish sources, most ferret owners advise staying away from fish-based diets because ferrets may not like them as much, and they tend to make the ferret's waste have more of an odor.

It's a very good idea to change your ferret's food from time to time to keep him from becoming so set in his ways that he refuses any change of kibble. In case your chosen food product goes off the market for some reason, or the manufacturer changes the recipe, get your ferret accustomed to occasional food changes. Any diet changes should be made over several weeks however, and you should gradually mix the new food with the old food until you've completely eliminated any of the old diet.

Your pet may find fruits tasty, but only as an occasional treat.

Vitamin supplements will benefit your pet.

Special Treats

Any treat, no matter how healthy, should be given in moderation. Instead of packaged treats that are sometimes high in sugar, there are vitamin supplements for ferrets, as well as hairball remedies that ferrets generally love. Besides being tasty, they provide a needed benefit. These make good training aids and treats but only should be given on occasion.

Other healthy treats that you can feed to your ferret include raisins, bananas, apples, cereals that are low in sugar and salt, eggs (hard boiled or scrambled, never raw), peanut butter, and cooked meats (chicken, beef, liver, etc.). These should all be fed in very small amounts, and no more than one or two small pieces per day.

Overfeeding your ferret treats may keep him from eating his regular kibble, which can upset his nutritional balance and weaken his immune system, and thus make him more susceptible to illness. Ferrets can't digest plant matter, and although your ferret may find raw vegetables and fruits tasty, they have no nutritional value.

> ### Water
>
> Your ferret must have access to fresh, clean water at all times, no matter what feeding routine you follow. Refill his water bottle every day and give it a good cleaning once a week.

Give treats in small amounts—only one or two pieces per day.

Part 2

Ferrets normally gain weight in winter, so make sure you provide plenty of exercise.

Fat Ferrets

Obesity is a common problem in ferrets. It can lead to many serious health issues and can even be fatal if allowed to continue unchecked. A lack of proper exercise is the leading cause of obesity in ferrets, although it's true that some ferrets are more prone to overeat than others.

The Obese Ferret

What you feed your ferret, how much, and how often will determine his weight. Just like humans, ferrets come in all different sizes and body shapes. A healthy adult male can be anywhere from two to five pounds, and a female will weigh about half that. Ferrets, especially males, normally gain more weight in the winter and then lose it again in the spring. Some ferrets just have a stockier built than others, too, which can make one appear heavier than another longer and leaner ferret.

When you run your hand down your ferret's side, you should feel his muscles ripple a bit and be able to feel the ribs, but they shouldn't stick out or feel too bony. Little "love handles" are common in the winter. If the ferret feels soft and "mushy" or looks pear-shaped, he might be overweight or just have poor muscle tone from insufficient exercise. Try letting him exercise more often and for longer periods of time, and try cutting back a bit on his food.

Just as an overweight, out-of-shape person doesn't feel as well as someone who is physically fit, your ferret may start to exhibit different emotional or behavioral problems as a result of being unfit.

Feeding the Sick Ferret

There are hundreds of recipes for nutritional supplements for ill ferrets. Many of these go by the name "duck soup" and are derived from a base of human nutritional supplements. These supplements contain a vast number of additives from brewer's yeast to heavy cream, to olive oil, and everything in between. Many veterinarians will also

Duck Soup

For a ferret that is recuperating from an illness, or an elderly ferret that needs special nutrition, most breeders and veterinarians suggest feeding a homemade "soup" that most refer to as "Duck Soup."

"Duck Soup"

1 can human nutrition supplement* (8 ounce)
1 can water (8 ounce)
2 scoops puppy or kitten weaning formula – (optional)
4 oz. dry kitten or ferret food, soaked in enough water to cover and soften it completely

*You can substitute ready-to-eat milk-replacement for kittens

Mix thoroughly. Feed at room temperature, about four fluid ounces at a time, twice a day for maintenance. If your ferret begins to gain too much weight too quickly, dilute the mixture with a bit of water.

This formula freezes well, so it's always a good idea to have a few days' supply in the freezer in case of emergency.

suggest treating sick ferrets with a liquid dietary supplement formulated for dogs and cats.

The following are some of the problems encountered with feeding these special supplement diets.

• They are time-consuming and expensive to prepare.

• There is often little scientific basis for the various additives you may find in them.

• They are generally fed in a liquid formulation via syringe by the owner.

Getting the Sick Ferret to Eat

If your ferret is sick and doesn't want to eat, you can try feeding him baby food. Chicken or chicken with broth is more nutritionally correct for an ailing ferret and more easily digestible than other meats and vegetables, although anything is better than nothing. A sick ferret that totally refuses food is a ferret in danger. Feed the ferret whatever you have to feed to get him to eat, but avoid fruit- or vegetable-based foods if possible.

While the first problem is just an inconvenience on the part of the pet owner, the second and third can actually be dangerous or even fatal to an ill animal. Not only can feeding the wrong diet actually weaken the system of an already ill animal, but forcing a weakened animal to take liquids by syringe can also result in accidental inhalation of the liquid, which, if it doesn't cause instant death, can cause pneumonia that often leads to death.

Baby Food

A simpler and safer method for feeding a sick ferret is to have him take baby or toddler food from your finger. Make sure that you buy a high-quality food with as high nutrition as possible. Feeding baby food to the ill ferret has proven to be a more than adequate temporary diet for ill or older ferrets that won't eat their normal ferret feeds. It is convenient, affordable, and most importantly, safe. This feeding trick has been proven over the years by research as well as general practice by veterinarians, breeders, and owners to be safe and effective.

"Finger food" can encourage picky ferrets to eat.

The baby food should be warmed to just slightly above room temperature. You can use a microwave or place the baby food jar in a pan of boiling water. Be sure to not overheat it, as overcooking reduces nutritional value in some foods. Check it with your finger to be sure there are no hot spots in the food.

In a best-case scenario, the ferret will be so thrilled by this exotic new scent that he'll dive headfirst into the jar and lick it clean. However, if he is too sick to pay attention to mundane matters such as food, you can try enticing him by putting a small amount on your finger and have him sniff it.

If the ferret still shows no interest in eating the food, gently pry open his mouth by placing your fingers on either side of the upper jaw and just behind his canine teeth. After gently (but firmly) prying the ferret's mouth open, place the baby food on the roof of the ferret's mouth. Your ferret may spit and may struggle a bit, but don't worry—he'll get plenty in. For some, that first taste is all it takes to jolt the taste buds into

Vitamin Supplements

If you feed your ferret a quality food, extra vitamin supplements are usually not required. You may find a supplement such as Ferretone™ or Linatone™ necessary as a training aid, however. Ferrets almost universally love the taste. (If your ferret doesn't seem willing to try it at first, place a drop on your finger and rub it in his mouth.) Ferretone™ and Linatone™ are very high in Vitamin A. Some breeders suggest reducing the amount of Vitamin A that their ferrets ingest by diluting the supplement with olive oil; one part supplement to two parts (or greater) olive oil. Give no more than a total of one-half teaspoon of the diluted supplement a day.

action. A good rule of thumb is to feed about one-fourth to one-fifth of a jar every three to four hours. When the ferret starts licking the food off your finger, you can give him as much as he wants at each feeding (or when he shows signs of appetite).

Weaning the Ferret off Baby Food

Once your ferret is back in good health, you may find that slathering yourself with baby food several times a day is less appealing to you than it is to your ferret. It's time to use the tough love theory and start your ferret back on a typical ferret diet. Although he'll likely complain loudly, a healthy ferret won't go without food for long. You don't want to force the issue by cutting him off of his special diet entirely, but when he feels well enough to complain about the service, he's well enough to start being treated like a normal ferret.

Start feeding the baby food only by spoon or saucer (being sure to thoroughly check for hot spots, especially if you heat the food in a microwave). Then you can begin gradually working the ferret back toward a balanced diet of dry kibble. Unless you're doing so under a vet's supervision, never keep a ferret on a diet that consists solely of baby food or any other non-approved diet for longer than three to four months. Although the ferret can exist quite nicely for this length of time, going any longer without a better nutritional balance can eventually cause more harm than good. While baby food is an excellent supplement and a good replacement for a regular diet for short-term feeding, baby food lacks the vitamins, minerals, and other compounds (most especially Taurine) that ferrets require for their long-term health.

Part 2

If you are still feeding the baby food after three to four weeks have passed, it's time to start adding a little bit of the ferret's usual kibble to somewhat balance the nutritional values. The easiest way to do this is to use a blender. Put the baby food into the blender, add a few kibbles, and let it grind away. You can gradually add more kibble until you are feeding more kibble than baby food.

At that time, you can usually put un-ground kibble in a bowl with some baby food on top, and the ferret will soon get used to eating the full-sized kibbles again.

Whether you're starting to feed a neglected ferret with a better quality food, starting a baby ferret on his permanent diet, or retraining a recuperating ferret to eat his dry food after

Generally Accepted Good Ingredients for Ferret Foods:

Remember that meat should always be the first item listed in the ingredients.

Meats

Turkey or turkey meal

Chicken or chicken meal

Lamb or lamb meal

Whole eggs

Liver or liver meal

Fish or fish meal (accepted but not suggested)

Note: Beef products are questionable because of digestibility as well as potential allergic reactions.

Fats

Chicken fat

Turkey fat

Poultry fat

Other

Beet pulp

Brewer's Yeast (which is a good Vitamin B supplement)

Nutritional Requirements for the Average Ferret

The following nutritional requirements can be used as a guide on what foods are appropriate for the average ferret. However, remember that growing kits and pregnant or nursing females will eat a lot more than your average ferret, so provide them with more than usual.

Protein: 32 to 38 percent
Fat: 18 to 25 percent
Carbohydrates: Simple carbs are preferred, with no sweets in the food
Starch: Well-cooked, extruded
Ash: Less than 7 percent
Moisture: Less than 12 percent

being spoiled with tempting treats while he was ill, make the change a little bit at a time so your ferret can adjust gradually.

Start adding the new food to your ferret's old food in a ratio of 90 percent old food to 10 percent new food. Then gradually over the period of a week or so increase the portion of new food(s) and decrease the portion of old foods until you're feeding the ferret 100 percent of his regular (or new) kibble. While you're making the change, keep an eye on your ferret's stool. Be sure your ferret is eating enough, that his stool stays firm, and that he isn't showing any signs of diarrhea or upset stomach.

Other than regular veterinary checkups, what you choose to feed your ferret will have more to do with how long and how healthy his life will be than any other decision you will make.

9

Litter Box Training

When you bring home your ferret, you'll likely have certain expectations regarding his behavior. One of the most common expectations is that the ferret is going to be like a cat and know instinctively where to go to the bathroom. Be forewarned that if you are expecting such dedication, you really should consider getting a cat instead. Don't expect your ferret to automatically realize what that box in the corner filled with pellets should be used for. Don't be surprised if he uses the litter for sleeping, playing, or for storing toys instead of what it was intended for. Unlike cats, who seem to be born knowing how and why to use a litter pan, for most ferrets, the litter box is either considered to be a large bed, a toy, a useless piece of plastic that

Ferrets must learn to use litter boxes.

must be pushed out of the corner to make room for bathroom visits or, in a last-case scenario, a bathroom.

Litter Box Habits

Ferrets are actually very clean and neat animals. They follow, at least to some extent, enough social etiquette to keep their bathroom area removed from their eating and sleeping areas. Ferrets are "latrine" animals. This means that they pick a spot and return to that spot time after time when they have to eliminate. They are naturally inclined to use corners as their bathroom of choice, however. This can create a problem in itself, as in almost every room, even in a typical four-sided cage, there are four corners. Multiply the multi-levels in a cage by those four corners, and you can see a problem pattern emerging. It can be quite frustrating to everyone involved to try to figure out in which corner to put the litter pan.

The first rule in successful litter training is to let the ferret choose his own bathroom location. You'll save countless hours of frustration by allowing the ferret to dictate his own preference in this instance, instead of trying to have him learn to use the litter box where you have placed it according to your preference.

Not only are there four corners in most rooms, but any piece of furniture located against a wall also creates two additional corners. With so many choices, it's inevitable that ferrets that have access to your entire house or an entire room will discover and use as bathrooms "corners" their humans have not previously considered as such. Again, the best way to avoid frustration on everyone's part is to allow the ferret to choose the location and simply place the litter box there, no matter how strange it may seem to you.

Let your pet choose his bathroom spot – then place the litter box.

Ferrets are likely to choose a corner to use as a restroom.

Once your ferret has decided on a location in his cage for the litter box, you need to attach the litter box securely in place. Some ferrets will push the pan out of the way so they can eliminate in the space behind it. Others will just enjoy playing with anything they find in their cage that will move if they push it. Dumping litter seems to be a favorite pastime of many younger ferrets. If you find it takes too much time to fasten and unfasten the pan with every cleaning, simply purchase two identical pans, attach one securely to the wire, and then just drop the other inside it.

The Litter

Now that you have the litter box in the right place, what type of litter do you plan to use? There are many types of litter on the market that are acceptable for ferrets. You can save money and the expense of searching out litter especially labeled for ferrets by buying cat litter. Any litter made from recycled newspaper or biodegradable grain products should work fine.

However, you should always stay away from cedar or "clumping" cat litters. Cedar has a resin that can be stirred up in the dust from the litter. This can cause respiratory problems in ferrets. Clumping cat litters are often much too dusty, and if the dust "clumps" in the ferret's respiratory passages, it can be fatal.

Litter can't be chosen just for its absorbency or other factors. It also should be dust-free. Since most ferrets like to dig their faces in their litter, they can get the litter and dust up their noses

Ferrets can use dust-free, non-clumping cat litter.

Toilet Training Tips

·Use a low-walled box litter box so your ferret can get in and out of it easily.

• Leave a little waste in the box to make it clear that it is the toilet area.

• Put lots of blankets and towels around the box to clearly separate the bathroom area.

• Constantly supervise the ferret while he is out of the cage during the early stages of toilet training.

Almost every ferret can be trained to use a litter pan.

Cleaning up Accidents

"Accident" corners should be cleaned very well using vinegar, diluted bleach, or any other disinfectant. (Remember to keep your ferret away from all cleaning chemicals.) A harsh-smelling cleaning product will prevent the area from smelling like a bathroom to your ferret, and will also act as a general deterrent. For that same reason, you shouldn't clean litter pans with bleach or other harsh detergents, and certainly do not use the same one that you're using as a deterrent elsewhere.

and into their eyes, causing irritation and sometimes infections. Always choose litters that are as dust-free as possible.

Correcting Mistakes

As smart as they are, ferrets make mistakes. And most of the mistakes will be about using the litter box–or rather not using it. If your ferret seems to be using everything in his cage except the litter box, try covering all the floor space with bedding, his food dish, and water bottle. Soon, he'll figure out what the box is actually for and you can begin taking up some of the bedding and give him a little more play area.

If you have a really large multi-level cage and you keep finding mistakes on levels other than the one with the litter box, you can either put a second pan in at a higher level, or take out some of the levels, forcing the ferret to remain in a smaller area, thus having to use the litter box. Putting a smaller pan on a higher level will sometimes work just as well as using another full-sized pan but will allow more space for maneuvering.

When ferrets are allowed to run loose in the house, they are far more likely to make mistakes than when confined to their cages. Most ferrets will make an effort to use the

A Second Litter Box

Plastic shoeboxes make good second litter boxes, and they have the added advantage of having a snap-on lid, which makes them excellent for use in a travel cage. This is also good to use if you're planning a trip to the vet. The vet can see for herself exactly what the stools look like and get a fresh stool sample without having to use a loop to get a sample from your ferret. To keep the litter box from turning over during travel, use self-stick tape to fasten a litter pan to the floor of the travel crate. Attach the loop side to the floor of the crate, and secure the hook side to the bottom of the litter box.

Having more than one pet may mean having more than one litter box.

litter pan when in the general vicinity of its location, but few will travel to another room to use one. It's a good idea to either keep your ferret confined to one smaller area of your house until you're sure he has the concept down pat, or be content to live with litter pans in every room. It may also help if you put a box of toys or some snuggly material (or old clothing) in corners you don't want the ferret to soil. Once the ferret has designated an area for sleeping or playing or eating, he will rarely, if ever, soil it again.

Some ferrets will seem to have the right idea and you'll proudly watch as your ferret heads to the corner with the litter box in it–only to see him go to the bathroom right next to the box! If this is a new pan that he hasn't used before, check to see if the sides of the pan are too high. If the sides of the pan are too high and the ferret can't see into the box, you have formed a "false corner" with the box, and the ferret is visualizing the side of the pan as part of the wall. You may want to cut down one side so that he can see the litter.

Why Did My Ferret Stop Using the Litter Box?

If your ferret has always been good with his toilet practices but suddenly stops using his litter box, your first concern should be his health. Take the ferret to the vet and have the vet do a complete exam. Once you've determined that it's not a medical problem causing the ferret to lose control of his bowels, look next to see if anything has changed in your

Litter Training in a Nutshell

·Initially, keep your ferret confined to his cage with a litter box.

• If your ferret seems to prefer another area of the cage, move the litter box there.

• Once your ferret is using the litter box in the cage, let the ferret out of the cage in a limited space, under close supervision. Place a second litter box outside of the cage in this space.

• Place the ferret in the litter box before taking him out to play and take him to the box during playtime.

• If you notice your ferret backing into a corner, take him to the litter box immediately.

• Whenever the ferret uses the litter box, make sure he gets lots of praise and a favorite treat.

• Never punish your ferret for mistakes.

• Add more litter boxes as necessary because a ferret likely won't go too far in search of a litter box.

• Be flexible about the placement of litter boxes. If your ferret seems to prefer a particular place as a toilet, put a box there.

• If your ferret begins having accidents, go back to the confinement or limited space with supervision stage and begin the training again.

house or in the ferret's daily routine. Have you moved the furniture around his cage, or in the room(s) where he has free access? Is there a new pet or a different person in the house? Has his schedule or your schedule changed? Any of these factors can change your ferret's bathroom habits.

Most of the time, simply giving the ferret a gentle reminder of where the litter box is can be enough to get him back into the box. Sometimes, if there is a new animal in the house, your ferret could be just expressing his displeasure at sharing your affection with someone else. If there is a new ferret in the house that is also using "his" litter box, you may have to get a second (or third) litter pan until the first ferret gets used to the "intruder." Some ferrets refuse to share their litter pans and you may need to keep separate litter boxes for your ferrets on a permanent basis.

Be Patient
Although almost every ferret can be trained to use a litter pan, there is individual variation.

Even the most well trained ferret will tend to lose track of his litter pans when frightened or excited or if he is in a new house or in a room. In general, you can expect at least a 90 percent "hit" rate, although some ferrets just don't catch on as well, and some do considerably better.

If it appears that your ferret has completely forgotten all about litter pans, you might need to retrain him by confining him to a smaller area or even a cage for a week or so and gradually expanding his space as he catches on again.

Waste Management

Common sense will tell you that the more frequently the litter box is cleaned out, the less noticeable the odor will be. Deciding how often to clean the litter box will depend on the number of ferrets using each litter pan. If the box is not cleaned frequently enough, your ferret may

Be patient. Every ferret responds differently to training.

Part 2

The Golden Rules of Litter Training

1. Remember that ferrets are creatures of habit. Let your ferret choose the location of the litter box in his cage. Watch your ferret to see which corner of the cage he prefers to use as a bathroom, and place his litter box in that corner.

2. Choose a litter box with sides at least four inches high to prevent the ferret from aiming over the edge of the box. You may need to put newspaper under the box to catch the inevitable misses.

3. Use a pelleted litter made from either wood or recycled newspaper. Clay litters and clumping cat litters are not recommended.

4. Attach the box firmly to the cage to prevent your ferret from dumping the contents.

5. Be ready to exercise plenty of patience. It takes some ferrets much longer than others to "catch on."

simply stop using the litter pan as a form of protest. Cleaning out the pan completely and starting over with new litter, then being fastidious about keeping it cleaned out on a daily basis, is always the first step in correcting bad litter training behavior patterns. Sprinkling a little bit of the old, "used" litter over the fresh litter in new or cleaned litter pans will remind your ferret that this is not a new sand box to play in.

The most important thing to remember when litter training a ferret is that each ferret is an individual, and will respond differently to different techniques and training methods. Just keep trying until you find the method that works best for the both of you.

10

Grooming Your Ferret

Unlike the responsibility of taking on a pet with long hair, such as a Persian cat or an Afghan hound, the grooming requirements for a ferret are actually quite simple. They are pretty much "wash and wear" animals, requiring very little to maintain their appearance. Brushing your ferret will help get rid of dead hairs and will keep his coat glossy and shiny, but it's not totally necessary as it is with many other pets.

Does My Ferret Need a Bath?

Frequent bathing is not recommended for ferrets, as it can actually make their normally slightly musky odor much stronger for a while. The average ferret can go about every four to six months between baths. Of course, excursions

Ferrets are pretty much "wash-and-wear" animals.

Though brushing isn't necessary, it keeps your pet's coat glossy.

When baths are mandatory, have everything ready before you begin.

into the fireplace, cake batter, or the flour bin can make these baths necessary more often. Sometimes young kits will require more frequent bathing than older ferrets until their body learns to regulate itself and their odor becomes more acceptable. Most experts agree that a ferret should never be bathed any more often than once a month. If your ferret has gotten into something messy and needs a bath, enlist a helper and be sure to have everything ready before you begin.

How to Bathe Your Ferret

You should use a good ferret-formulated shampoo for normal bathing; however, a "no-tears" shampoo made for babies can be used if you are concerned about getting shampoo in the ferret's eyes (and thus making him hate bathtime even more than he does already). Human and canine shampoos are much too harsh for ferret coats and skin, so don't be tempted to use them when you're bathing your ferret. If you have to use a flea shampoo, never use a regular dog or cat shampoo (or worse, flea and tick dip or powder). Always use kitten-safe shampoo. If you have concerns or questions about the type or brand of shampoo to use on your ferret, consult your veterinarian.

The bath and rinse water should be warm, but not hot. When you're testing the water temperature, remember that a ferret's body temperature is about four degrees higher than a human's, so what feels lukewarm to you, will feel somewhat cold to the ferret. A double basin sink works well as a "ferret bathtub." Fill one side with a few inches of warm water for rinsing, and use the other side for the wash and scrub operation. A plastic dishpan or a large mixing bowl will work almost as well. Fill the

Part 2

Bathing Supplies

You will need to purchase a good ferret shampoo and some odor eliminator products. No matter how clean and tidy you keep your ferret, he is going to have a somewhat musky odor. There are several sprays on the market that you can use when company is coming to make your ferret more appealing to a non-ferret-person's nose. Ferrets don't need regular baths, but you should be prepared to bathe him after he's crawled into a potted plant to do some gardening. Keep all your old towels for ferret bedding and for ferret bathtime.

Young kits tend to require more bathing than adult ferrets.

basins before you put the ferret into it. The running water may frighten the ferret, although many ferrets may learn to actually like the feel of the water running gently over them as they're being rinsed.

Once you've gotten the ferret thoroughly wet, apply the shampoo. Remember, it does no good to use warm water if you shock your poor ferret's system by pouring icy cold shampoo onto him. Either place the shampoo bottle into a pan of hot water to warm it up or squirt some into your hands and hold it until it warms up. Work the shampoo into a lather. Don't forget to wash the head and tail, and get under the legs.

Gently dip the ferret into rinse water and rinse him thoroughly. A sink sprayer sometimes works wonders, but it will frighten some ferrets. If you're going to try using the sprayer, start slowly with the

Remember to wash the tail and under the legs.

Use water that will feel warm to the ferret.

water on a very weak stream and gradually turn the water on higher pressure. Repeat the sudsing and rinsing as needed. A few drops of moisturizer oil added to the final rinse water will help prevent the ferret's skin from drying out. You can also spray on an oil and water mixture and rub it in thoroughly after the final rinse.

If you are using a kitten-safe flea shampoo, always start at the neck and work toward the tail to prevent the fleas from migrating from the body upward. Be extremely careful around the eyes. Ferrets are fast learners and may learn from one experience that bath time means pain or discomfort. Try to make their first few baths as pleasant as possible. Some

Bath Tips

- Give your ferret some time out of his cage before bathing him. Let him use the litter box and settle down a little before attempting a bath.

- Have everything you need ready before you start bathing your ferret.

- Do not bathe your ferret too frequently. Ferrets should be bathed no more than once a month.

- Only a ferret shampoo, kitten shampoo, or no-tears baby shampoo should be used to bathe your ferret.

- Kitten-safe flea shampoo can be used, with care. Never use dog or cat flea shampoos, or flea collars, powders, or dips on a ferret.

- Ferrets prefer their baths rather warm. If the water feels lukewarm to you, it's probably cold to your ferret.

- Take care not to frighten your ferret with running water or sprays.

- Ferrets can be bathed in a sink, a dishpan, a clean litter pan, a bathtub, or directly under the faucet.

- Remember to warm the shampoo before applying it onto the ferret.

- Towel dry your ferret to remove excess water, and then put him in a confined area with a pile of clean, dry towels.

- Some ferrets will tolerate being dried off with a hairdryer on the very lowest/coolest setting.

Hair, There, Everywhere!

The ferret usually sheds his coat twice a year—in the late winter or early spring, and in the late summer or early fall. Ferrets groom themselves fairly well, so daily brushing is not necessary, but it is helpful. During the self-grooming time, the ferret may ingest significant amounts of hair and this can cause an upset stomach and even serious intestinal blockages. Therefore, a little bit of a hairball remedy paste (about half an inch or so) made for cats should be given daily or every other day through the shedding period to help prevent a blockage. If you suspect a hair blockage, contact the vet immediately. Substances such as vegetable or mineral oils will not break up hairballs.

Have plenty of towels on hand for drying time.

ferrets will enjoy paddling around in a bathtub with just a couple of inches of warm water, merrily chasing their toys and ducking into the water and diving for heavier objects. Let the ferret get used to water by allowing him plenty of tub time, and you'll make bath time more pleasurable for the both of you!

Make sure that you have plenty of towels handy when bathtime is over. Rub the ferret's fur reasonably dry, then put your ferret into a box or travel cage with several more dry towels and he will finish the drying job himself.

Hard as Nails

Your ferret's toenails will have to be trimmed about once a week or once every other week throughout your ferret's life. If you don't keep the nails well trimmed, the nails will grow

Trim your ferret's nails with a regular, human-type toenail clipper at least once a week.

Declawing?

Even if you could find a veterinarian willing to do the surgery, you should never consider declawing a ferret. They need their nails like you need the ends of your fingers and toes. This practice is cruel and inhumane to the ferret and should not be done under any circumstances.

to painful length and the vein in the nail will expand downward and make future trimming difficult (and potentially harmful). The front nails usually have to be trimmed more frequently than the rear ones.

Use a regular human-type toenail clipper to cut your ferret's nails. (The dog/cat type will work but is more difficult to use and also tends to split the nail.) Make sure that the clipper is sharp; otherwise, it can cause the nail to splinter.

Clip the nails so that the flat portion of the trimmed nail will be parallel to the floor when the ferret is walking. A couple of quick strokes with an emery board to round off the edges of the nail after clipping will also prevent further splitting and will make the nail smoother and less likely to snag on things (such as your skin or the carpet).

You'll quickly find out that getting his toenails clipped isn't even close to being in the top ten of your ferret's list

A tasty liquid treat will distract a wriggly pet during nail clipping.

of "fun things to do." He will wriggle, squirm, twist, pull, and do anything he can to escape from your grip. A much easier way than wrestling him into submission (hard to do with a ferret, as you'll learn) is to lay the ferret on your lap with his head up and his back toward you, and place a few drops of vitamin supplement or another treat on his stomach. Show the ferret the treat and then, while he is busy snacking, start clipping.

When you trim the nails, look carefully for the dark vein, or the "quick" of the nail. Be careful that you do not clip into this vein. It is a good idea to have styptic powder handy just in case, because if you do clip into this vein, the nail is going to bleed. Apply the styptic powder to stop the bleeding.

Ear and There

There will normally be a buildup of a reddish wax in a ferret's ear that should be removed about once a month. One of the best ways to clean the ears is to let the ferret do most of the work. Drop some ear cleaning medicine deep into the ear and massage it for a few moments. Then let the ferret shake his head. Most of the earwax will be shaken out, and what's left on the surface can be easily removed with a cotton ball.

If the wax is a dark gray or black and the ear has an unpleasant odor, it is likely that ear mites are present. Have your vet examine the ferret and make a diagnosis. Commercial

To properly groom your ferret you'll need the following supplies:

- Ear wash or baby oil
- Gentle slicker brush
- Ferret shampoo (or human baby shampoo)
- Flea and tick shampoo designed for ferrets
- Deodorizing spray or cologne
- Small pet nail trimmers
- Cotton balls
- Old towels
- Hairball remedy (or petroleum jelly)

Clean your pet's ears about once a month.

Cleaning ferret teeth is best left to a veterinarian.

over-the-counter ear mite products will work eventually, but your veterinarian has medications that will work much quickly and more effectively. Be sure to clean the ears thoroughly before using any of the ear mite medicines.

Other causes of excessive wax and ear scratching are bacterial or fungal infections. This is why a vet should examine your ferret in the case of a possible infection, so that he or she can administer or recommend the proper treatment.

Sink Your Teeth into It

Like any other mammal's teeth, ferrets' teeth can build up a layer of tarter that, if left untreated, will eventually lead to tooth and gum disease. Feeding your ferret a dry ferret food and keeping sugary treats to a minimum will help keep the rate of tarter buildup low. Eventually though, even with proper maintenance, your ferret's teeth will take on a yellowish hue, sometimes with brown spots, and it will be time for a cleaning.

Although some experienced ferret owners claim to have great success cleaning the ferret's teeth at home, unless you have some dental experience, you should probably leave this job to the professionals. Most people would not know how (or want to try) to hold a squirming, wriggling, unhappy ferret while attempting to scrape the ferret's teeth up under the gum line with a sharp dental tool.

Not only can a veterinarian clean your ferret's teeth, but she will also know what else to look for, such as cracked or broken teeth (especially canines) or indications of a gum abscess. The teeth should be scaled well up under the gum line where hidden tartar could cause serious gum diseases over time. A deep cleaning such as this is usually done under a general anesthetic (isoflorane is preferred). Most vets will also polish the teeth after the cleaning is done, scaling them in order to seal the surface of the teeth against decay.

A well-groomed ferret is a happy ferret. Use your grooming time to check over your

Part 2

ferret's body for new lumps or bumps that could be early warning symptoms of illness or injury. Early detection is the key to keeping your pet healthy. With proper training, grooming time can become a bonding experience for you and your ferret.

Part 2

Part Three

Your Ferret at Home

"You youngsters think you have it tough. Back in my day,
we didn't have plastic running balls, we used cubes."

Ferret Health Care

Keeping your ferret healthy requires more than just a bit of work on your part. How sensitive you are to your ferret's normal actions and reactions can literally make the difference between life and death for your ferret. Being your ferret's best friend will not only warm the cockles of your heart and enrich your life, but will also mean that you will be more in-tune to his emotions and physical actions and reactions than will someone who merely exists in the same home with their pet. You will find that it doesn't take a pet psychic to tell when something is bothering your furry friend once you have familiarized yourself with his routines, his play behavior, and his daily routines. Something that might have gone unnoticed to a less-caring pet owner will send

Ferrets are generally healthy animals.

you racing to the vet at the first hint of a possible health problem. Most veterinarians will tell you that the most important aspect of your ferret's health care will be the care that your provide on a daily basis.

Your sensitivity to your ferret's behavior can save his life.

Vaccinations

Vaccines are extremely important for your ferret and should be administered exactly on the schedule suggested when you purchase him. Most breeders and veterinarians suggest giving a distemper booster at 8 weeks, repeated at 11-12 weeks and then at 14-16 weeks; thereafter they should receive a booster on an annual basis.

The rabies shot should be administered at 12-13 weeks of age (two weeks before/after the distemper, but never at the same time) and then given annually.

There are two canine distemper vaccines that can be used, Fervac-D (the only USDA approved-for-ferrets shot), or Galaxy-D. Although the number of cases of a ferret contracting, passing, or carrying rabies is just about non-existent, and the rabies shot is not always required by law, there is one ferret-approved rabies vaccine called IMRAB-3. This is one shot that could save your ferret's life in case of a ferret bite or scratch that gets reported to the authorities. Unfortunately, there are still a large number of states that will confiscate your ferret for rabies testing, despite the 1998 Compendium of Animal Rabies Control by the Centers for Disease Control and Prevention stating that the animal should be quarantined for ten days. If you travel with your ferret, be sure that you carry proof of rabies immunization with you at all times.

Vaccines are extremely important to your pet.

Vaccine Reactions

Severe reactions to vaccinations occur more frequently in ferrets than in other domesticated animals. This can range from mild facial swelling, to severe swelling, vomiting, diarrhea, and death if not treated immediately. The following steps should be taken to prevent a severe vaccination reaction in your ferret.

• Notify the veterinarian before vaccination if your ferret has had previous vaccine reactions, and be prepared to stay at the clinic for 20 to 30 minutes after vaccinations are administered.

• Pre-medication before vaccination is often helpful and is recommended for ferrets that have previously had vaccine reactions.

• Administering vaccines separately and allowing at least several days to one week between vaccines will help reduce the risk of a reaction.

Experts do not recommend avoiding vaccines as an alternative to vaccine reactions. Distemper in ferrets is almost always fatal, whereas vaccine reactions can be treated and very few are fatal when treatment is started early in the vaccine reaction.

Common Ferret Ailments

Ferrets are prone to many different types of health problems, and it's a good idea to take your ferret for regular veterinary checkups to find any potential problems before they become untreatable or require more drastic treatments.

While a young ferret may need to go to the vet only on an annual basis, barring emergency or illness, it is recommended that once a ferret reaches the age of three years, he begins a six-month checkup regimen. The ferret should have blood workups done annually to screen for disease as well as to give your vet a baseline for what is "normal" for that particular animal. Most diseases common to ferrets are treatable if caught early enough. Although the extra tests may seem costly, it can

Most diseases common to ferrets are treatable if caught early.

actually save you money in the long run if you avoid lengthy hospital stays and surgery later.

Although ferrets are basically healthy animals, they can be prone to any number of diseases and illnesses. It's very important that you learn how to recognize symptoms of serious illness or disease and know what to expect as the treatment. Some of the most common ailments include intestinal disorders, insulinomas, adrenal disease, lymphosarcoma, skin tumors, kidney disease, and cardiac disease.

Lethargy and loss of appetite may indicate your pet isn't feeling well.

Intestinal Disorders and Blockages

These disorders are often caused by the ingestion of foreign objects. Ingestion of foreign objects is most common in the young ferret, and hairballs are more common in the older ferret. Ferrets are very curious creatures, and they love to eat pencil erasers, marbles, and a myriad of other objects they should not eat. Pretty much anything that is small enough to swallow and doesn't try to eat him first is fair game for a ferret. If he sees it, in his mouth it goes.

If your ferret swallows a foreign object, veterinary attention needs to be sought immediately. Signs of foreign object ingestion include loss of appetite, diarrhea, lethargy, and sometimes vomiting. Very rarely will a ferret pass foreign objects unassisted. Unfortunately, surgical removal of the foreign object is usually necessary. However, the earlier the problem is dealt with, the faster your ferret should bounce back after surgery. Don't wait until he is so debilitated that he is in even more danger of dying due to increased weakness on the table during surgery.

Epizootic Catarrhal Enteritis (Green Slime Disease)

This is a highly infectious disease of the gastrointestinal tract often leading to a large amount of green, mucus-type diarrhea. This disease is usually seen in ferrets that are new in the house (sometimes called "stress diarrhea") or have recently been housed with strange ferrets. Any ferret showing this symptom should immediately be quarantined away from your other ferrets.

Part 3

The suggested treatment is to use aggressive supportive care (IV fluids, nutritional support, etc.) to keep the ferret strong, and the virus will have to pass on its own. Ferrets also commonly develop intestinal inflammation (enteritis) leading to diarrhea.

Veterinary care should be sought immediately whenever diarrhea is present in more than one stool, as ferrets will dehydrate very quickly. Until you can get to a veterinarian, try to rehydrate your ferret by giving him fluids with electrolytes. Many times, it is the best course of action to do nothing for diarrhea other than to keep your ferret well hydrated (drinking plenty of fluids). Sometimes diarrhea is nature's way of eliminating toxins from the system, and by stopping the diarrhea, you could be trapping the toxins inside the body, where they will grow and continue to do damage. Let your veterinarian decide what the best treatment is for your particular case.

Insulinoma /Hypoglycemia

Insulinomas are common in ferrets over two years of age. An insulinoma is a tumor in the pancreas, which causes it to secrete extra insulin, causing the glucose in the blood to drop. Signs of insulinoma include decreased activity, increased sleeping, weakness in the back legs, hyper salivation, and sometimes pawing at the mouth. High insulin levels will depress blood sugar levels to the point of collapse and coma. Immediate treatment is directed toward stabilizing blood sugar levels and providing blood pressure support if necessary. Long-term care requires treatment of the underlying cause. Routinely, patients with insulinoma are treated with corticosteroids (Prednisone) as a chemotherapy protocol.

Adrenal Disease

Another common and potentially fatal problem is adrenal disease. The adrenal gland grows in size and causes abnormal amounts of adrenal hormones to enter the bloodstream. Symptoms include hair loss, scratching, and swollen vulvas in females. This disease is commonly seen in ferrets around two to three years of age. The best treatment for

Scratching can be a symptom of many things and you will want to investigate its cause.

Check your ferret's eyes and nose for discharge that could indicate illness.

Aleutian Disease

Aleutian Disease is also referred to as the "ferret wasting disease." It was first seen in the mink in the 1940s, and didn't make its appearance in ferrets until the 1960s. It is often misdiagnosed, and can be fatal if not diagnosed and treated correctly. Symptoms include a black, tarry stool, paralysis, tremors and convulsions, as well as anorexia, weight loss, and lethargy.

adrenal tumors is surgery. Without surgery, adrenal tumors are quite often fatal.

Lymphosarcoma

Lymphosarcoma is another common disease of ferrets that may be seen in young or older ferrets. Signs include decreased activity, weight loss, appetite loss, respiratory distress, and enlarged lymph nodes. Chemotherapy is usually the preferred treatment. While there is a fair amount of literature available on this disease, we actually know very little about the causes.

Mast Cell Tumors

Although the very name mast cell tumors sounds frightening, these growths are actually benign (not dangerous). Unfortunately, they're not symptom-free, because these cells release histamines and cause intense itching. The tumors look like scabs, but they don't go away the way scabs will. Surgical removal is the only available treatment.

Canine Distemper

The next time you put off getting your ferret his annual vaccinations, remember that you're taking his life in your hands by doing so. While rabies is rare in ferrets, canine distemper is not. Canine distemper is almost 100 percent fatal in ferrets within 12 to 42 days after

Part 3

Canine Distemper Vaccinations

Ferret kits receive immunity from canine distemper from their mother, provided she was properly vaccinated. To maintain that immunity, kits need a series of three shots at 6, 10, and 14 weeks followed by a yearly booster. Adults only need a yearly booster unless you are unable to establish that the ferret has had previous vaccinations. Two shots given three to four weeks apart are recommended for adult ferrets that have not previously established and maintained immunity.

Currently, the only canine distemper (CD) vaccine tested and labeled for ferrets is a modified-live vaccine called Fervac-D. Another vaccine that has been used for many years on ferrets (but not labeled for ferrets) is Galaxy-D.

Remain at your vet's office for at least 30 minutes after your ferret receives any vaccination and watch for signs of anaphylaxis, such as sneezing, vomiting, hives, itching, swelling, bloody diarrhea, cessation of breathing, or collapse. Immediate veterinary care is necessary to save the life of a ferret that experiences anaphylactic shock including administering epinephrine, steroids, fluids, and antihistamines. If your ferret has a reaction, ask the veterinarian about pre-medicating your ferret prior to the next booster.

exposure. Once a ferret gets the disease, euthanasia is usually recommended to prevent the spread of the disease to other animals and end the animal's suffering.

Some of the signs of canine distemper include: loss of appetite, foul-smelling yellow or green sticky eye discharge, swollen eyelids, green or yellow nasal discharge, swelling of the lips and chin, thick brown crusts that form on the eyes, nose, lips and chin, lethargy, diarrhea, difficulty breathing, dehydration, convulsions, and, in the later stages, a thickening and hardening of the paw pads.

Many of these symptoms are never seen because the ferret will often die before the disease reaches an advanced stage. Ferrets do not appear to be susceptible to panleukopenia, or feline distemper.

You may think that because your ferret doesn't ever leave the house, he cannot be infected. This type of thinking is wrong. Canine distemper is an airborne virus that can be transmitted from direct or indirect contact with an infected animal. It can be carried on

Part 3

Gastric Ulcers

Ferrets can get ulcers almost exactly like the kind humans are prone to get. And, just as in humans, the ulcers can be caused by emotional and physical stress. Ferrets can get ulcers from a bacterium similar to human *H. pylori*, called *H. mustelae*. The treatment is similar to human treatment as well—antibiotics and a bland diet until the system returns to normal.

your clothing, shoes, or on your skin for at least eight hours after exposure. In other words, your ferret can become infected just by inhaling the virus from your skin or clothing.

Because the incubation period for canine distemper can be as long as 10 days, always isolate any new dogs or ferrets brought into your household for 14 days unless immunity to canine distemper (and other contagious illnesses) can be ascertained. Use caution and common sense when handling other dogs or ferrets. Be sure that any puppy that comes into your home or near you or your ferret has been properly vaccinated and checked by a veterinarian for signs of distemper. If you own a dog, be sure you keep it properly vaccinated for your ferret's sake, as well as the dog's good health.

Kidney and Cardiac Problems

Kidney and cardiac problems are also common in the ferret. Kidney disease can be recognized by increased water consumption and increased urination. Heart disease is most common in middle aged and older ferrets. Cardiac disease symptoms include weight loss, coughing, exercise intolerance, labored respiration, or shortness of breath. Treatment is directed to simultaneously improve pulmonary function and cardiac function. The long-term prognosis is poor.

Urethral Obstruction

Urethral obstructions are most common in male ferrets. They are often seen in conjunction with prostatic enlargement due to adrenal gland disease and can also be caused by urinary stones, infections, etc. Initial treatment is to relieve the obstruction with a urinary catheter. Further treatment includes fluid replacement, correction of electrolyte imbalances, and treatment of the infection.

Anal Prolapse

This is an emergency condition that is signaled by a ferret sliding across the floor, dragging his rear end, and sometimes whimpering in pain. It can be caused by the *E. coli* bacteria that can be transmitted from human to ferret and vice versa. It can be treated by medication prescribed by a veterinarian.

When Odd Behavior is a Medical Symptom

Symptom	Possible Causes
Lethargy	Anemia, low glucose, old age, heart disease, illness
Listing to one side	Ear infection, ear mites, stroke
Walking in Circles	Stroke
Excessive Grooming	tress, adrenal disease
Biting when Startled	Blind, deaf
Biting other ferrets	Blind, puberty in an un-sterilized ferret

Heartworms

Although heartworms are parasites and not a disease, they affect the heart adversely and can be fatal if not treated. The number of heartworm cases seen each year in ferrets is increasing, especially in the southern states. Ask your veterinarian about heartworm preventative medicine, especially if your ferret spends any time outdoors.

Colds and Allergies

Ferrets have a very weak immune system and can catch a cold or the flu from members of their human family, other animals, or airborne germs. Ferrets can also suffer from allergies. A head cold that might keep you out of work or school for a couple of days can prove fatal to a ferret. Always keep away from your ferret if you have any sort of influenza or virus.

If your ferret has excess discharge from his nose, you can wipe it with a tissue to help the ferret breathe and swallow. Running a cool mist

Ferrets can catch colds from members of their human family.

Part 3

Medication

Even if you are certain that you know what is wrong with your ferret, you should never give him any medication that has not been prescribed by your veterinarian. Medication that can cure problems in humans or other species can be fatal to ferrets. Dosages differ from species to species, and some human medications are extremely toxic to ferrets, even in very small doses.

humidifier near his cage, or placing your ferret in a travel cage inside a steamy bathroom will also help to loosen up mucus in the lungs, throat, and nose. If the cold lasts a couple of days, and your ferret is off his food more than usual, you may need a visit to the veterinarian for antibiotics.

Other Health Concerns
Temperature Tantrums

Whether you're in a car or in your house, it's always important to remember that ferrets don't handle changes in temperature the same way people do. Because ferrets originally lived in a cooler climate and in underground burrows that were protected from the heat, they do not tolerate heat as well as animals that evolved in warmer climates.

A ferret that starts displaying erratic or unacceptable behavior during summer months may simply be expressing his displeasure at being overly warm. Just as humans more easily lose their tempers when they are hot and sweaty, so will your ferret be more likely to snap when he is uncomfortably warm.

Unacceptable behavior in summer may be a "temperature tantrum."

Ferrets seem to be most comfortable in temperatures at about 65° F but can do fine in temperatures up to 75°. In temperatures above 80°, however, they will get uncomfortable. Temperatures above 85° can cause medical problems within hours, and temperatures over 90° can be fatal within a very short period of time. Older ferrets are more sensitive to heat than younger ferrets. Ferrets can survive prolonged periods of uncomfortable temperatures, but heat distress will eventually cause strain to the ferret's system. In cases of repeated heat stress, the immune system can be permanently compromised, making him susceptible to illness and disease.

Part 3

Act Fast!

Because ferrets are so small and have fast metabolisms, they can become seriously ill very quickly. The good news is that because you're a responsible pet owner who cares about your pet, you'll notice any symptoms of illness quickly and get your ferret proper health care. Keep in mind that just as quickly as they can get sick, ferrets that receive prompt medical attention are capable of recuperating fast.

Cooling off your ferret

The primary reason that our domestic ferrets have problems with higher temperatures is that they do not sweat. Humans perspire in hot weather, and the evaporation of that sweat helps cool us down. Ferrets aren't capable of doing this, nor do they pant as dogs do to move air over the moisture in their mouths to cool themselves. By the time a ferret begins to pant, he is in serious distress, and in danger of severe heatstroke. Immediate and drastic measures should be taken to bring his body temperature back down to the normal range.

Cool the ferret down steadily and slowly, and not suddenly. If the ferret becomes too cold too fast, he could easily continue the downward spiral even after he reaches the goal temperature. This can cause him to end up in worse distress than he was from the heat.

If your ferret goes into heat distress, you should cool him down by using tepid, not cold water. Cold water can easily put your ferret into shock, which can be more dangerous than the heat prostration. Submerge your ferret supporting his body just below the surface of the water (being sure to keep his head out of the water) until he is soaking wet. The ferret can then be put near a fan or a breeze to cool off after he is wet.

Never try to force-feed your ferret cold water in an attempt to cool him down because your ferret may inhale the water and choke. If tepid water is not available, place your ferret flat on his belly on a cold surface such as a dry bathtub, or cement floor, as these surfaces are usually cool. You should notice an improvement in your ferret fairly quickly. If no positive changes are noticeable, take your ferret to a vet immediately. You should allow your ferret free access to water once he is able to walk and is showing no further signs of distress. After his body temperature has returned to normal, let your veterinarian check him out to make sure no lasting damage was done.

Part 3

Cleanliness Counts

A clean living environment is a very important part of keeping your ferret healthy. Ferrets eat often and tend to eliminate frequently; therefore, the litter box needs to be scooped daily and scrubbed down weekly. Ferrets are very sensitive to many chemicals, so be cautious when choosing your household cleaners.

Because ferrets snack all day long, it is necessary to keep their food bowl constantly full. It is also necessary to clean out these food bowls at least once a week (most are dishwasher safe on the top rack) because of the grime that tends to build up on the bowl.

Parasites
Ticks and Fleas

If your ferret takes walks outdoors or comes near any animal that goes outdoors, there's a possibility that he could pick up a tick. Just what does a tick do? When a tick first finds your ferret, it attaches with its mouthpieces and begins to suck blood. When the tick gets "full," it regurgitates some blood back into the ferret, which is the point at which diseases are transmitted. The regurgitation usually happens between 5 and 24 hours after the tick attaches. The key to keeping your ferret healthy is early removal of ticks (using proper methods to avoid regurgitation)–and using proper prevention.

If you find a tick attached to your ferret, don't just grab hold and rip it off. The tick's head can break off and be left with embedded mouthparts in your ferret. This can cause skin infections and, worse, leave your ferret susceptible to many tick-borne diseases. Ticks are oxygen breathers, and you should suffocate them by dripping olive oil or putting a dab of petroleum jelly directly on them. As the tick struggles for air, it will start to release its grasp. Using tweezers or a tick puller, slowly and steadily draw the tick away from your ferret. Don't twist or squeeze the body of the tick, as this could push diseased blood back into your ferret.

Fleas don't carry the diseases that ticks can carry, such as Lyme disease or Rocky Mountain Spotted Fever, but they are pesky nonetheless. Ferrets never seem to have to give much thought to a reason for scratching in the first place, so having a flea walking around on their skin, biting their skin, and injecting irritants beneath the skin is enough to send even the most quiet ferret into paroxysms of itching and scratching, which can lead to skin infections and severe irritations.

Aside from using ferret-safe topical sprays and drops on your ferret to kill and deter fleas, you can use a premise spray directly around the cage, but you'll likely find you'll have to treat the entire house as well. Get a flea "bomb" that contains Methoprene (a flea growth regulator) that will interrupt the growth cycles. Of course, you will have to remove the ferrets from the house while you're spraying or bombing. Before you set off the bombs, make sure you wash all of the ferret's bedding in hot water and vacuum the area.

While you should never use flea or tick dips, collars, or powders formulated for dogs, cats, or other household pets, you can use repellent sprays labeled safe for kittens.

Heartworms

Fleas and ticks aren't the only external parasites that can cause problems for ferrets. Heartworms are transmitted by mosquitoes and are always fatal in ferrets. Even if your ferret never ventures outside, he may still be susceptible. You should consult your veterinarian about preventive measures and to see how severe the problem is in your particular area.

Home Health Care

Most veterinarians will agree that the health care that your ferret receives at home is far more important than the few times a year when the ferret visits the veterinarian. Be sure that you know the warning signs to look for in all major illnesses and that you quarantine any new ferrets coming into your home for the period of time recommended by your veterinarian. Make sure that you have ferret-proofed your home and are aware of danger signs of an intestinal blockage from a swallowed object, and keep your ferret on the suggested vaccination schedule.

Keeping a happy, healthy ferret isn't always easy, but it will always be rewarding!

Part 3

Emergency Care for Your Ferret

When you first bring home that energetic and playful ferret, it is hard to imagine him ever being ill or hurt. Certainly it is to be hoped that nothing will happen, but just as you keep aspirin or other remedies in your own medicine cabinet in case of a headache or illness, it is wise to be prepared to care for your ferret's illnesses ahead of time.

Every pet owner should have an emergency kit. At one time in your life you will probably face an emergency with your ferret, and it's far better to be safe than sorry. The most important item to have in your kit is an index card with all the pertinent ferret health care numbers on it. It should include your regular veterinarian, an emergency vet, and

It is wise to be prepared for ferret medical emergencies ahead of time.

First-Aid Kit

You should create an emergency first-aid kit and keep it on hand at all times. Most people use a fishing tackle box, or a plastic shoebox for the kit. Be sure that it contains the following:

Infant electrolyte fluid

Adult dietary supplement

Large infant medicine dropper (5 ccs) or infant medicine syringe

Honey, corn syrup, or other easily digestible nutrient source

Infant rectal thermometer

Heating pad

Small sturdy carrier with clean, warm, snuggly bedding in it

Antibacterial ointment

Hydrogen peroxide

Hemostats/scissors

Alcohol and betadine pads

Gauze sponges, a roll of gauze, tongue depressor, and bandaging tape

Cotton balls and cotton swabs

Jar of baby food (chicken), cat food, or other tasty treat for tempting a finicky eater

Eye flush

Hairball laxative

Nail clippers

Styptic powder

an animal poison control number. Armed with those numbers, you can get help for your ferret in almost any situation, at any time of day or night.

Although ferrets are usually very healthy creatures, there are still many causes for a ferret to become ill–from a simple head cold (perhaps caught from one of his humans) to ingesting something that won't pass through the digestive tract–or a variety of other problems. Whenever your ferret first shows signs of illness or lethargy or is not eating, drinking or eliminating, it is imperative to get him to his veterinarian at once.

Get a Pulse

It's simple to check your ferret's pulse rate. Press your fingertips on each side of his chest, count for ten seconds, and then multiply by six to get the rate per minute. The normal heart rate for a ferret is 120 beats per minute.

Contact your vet if your pet isn't eating, drinking, or eliminating.

Ferrets have rapid metabolisms and they can quickly become dehydrated if they are not eating or drinking as usual. In these cases, unless you can get to your vet immediately, start trying to rehydrate your ferret before you leave with him for the vet appointment. Know that several hours might be crucial however, especially if you are not sure when your ferret stopped drinking.

Accidents can happen to all of us, and to some, watching a ferret careening through the house in an ecstasy of joy, they seem at times to literally be an accident waiting to happen. Thus, it's very wise to be prepared for eventual injuries.

Be Prepared

Write down your regular veterinarian's telephone number and office hours on a card and keep it posted near your phone. Find out who covers for your vet when she is not available to be sure that person is also well equipped to handle a ferret emergency. Also find out who else in the area is knowledgeable in ferret emergency care. If you have a regular emergency care

Find out if the nearest emergency vet handles ferret emergencies.

It's possible to hydrate a debilitated ferret at home.

facility that will accept ferret clients in your area, keep that telephone number handy, along with directions on how to get to the clinic.

Emergency Problems and Solutions
Dehydration

Although it's not really simple to hydrate a debilitated ferret at home, it's not impossible. Mix equal parts adult dietary supplement and infant electrolyte fluid and draw the mixture up into either a large syringe or a medicine dropper. A ferret that has already lost the desire for any food or liquid may refuse the mixture. It is better to give many small doses than to overdo with one feeding and perhaps cause an upset stomach, especially if your ferret will soon be taking a car trip to the vet (which might cause him to become carsick). If your ferret doesn't seem interested in taking the mixture, you can place a few drops of the liquid in his cheek pocket and see if he swallows it. If he does, repeat this a few times. If your ferret refuses this mixture completely, or if he is vomiting, take him to an emergency clinic or to your veterinarian immediately.

Shock

Temperature is very important in the ill or injured ferret. A ferret that has been injured is likely to go into shock, and thus his body temperature can decrease rapidly. If you use a heating pad to maintain his body temperature, be sure it is kept on the lowest setting and is well covered by soft bedding. Even an ill ferret may chew or claw at the bedding, so be sure that the heating pad doesn't become damaged to the point of exposing wiring. Place the heating pad in the bottom of a box or basket. Put a blanket or towel around the heating pad to prevent the pad from burning the

What's Normal?

Knowing the normal vital signs for your ferret can help determine if he is going into shock, or needs even more immediate care.

Normal temperature is 100° to 102.5°F

Normal heart rate for a calm ferret is 120 beats per minute

Normal heart rate for a stressed ferret is 250 beats per minute

Normal respiratory rate is 30 to 40 breaths per minute.

ferret. Also wrap a blanket or towel around the box or blanket to keep out drafts.

Shock can occur after an injury or a severe scare. Other causes of shock are hemorrhaging, fluid loss, infection, poison, adrenal insufficiency, cardiac failure, and anaphylaxis. The symptoms of shock are a weak or rapid pulse, dilated pupils, shallow breathing, and muscle weakness. Time can be very critical to survival for shock treatment.

Broken Bones

If your ferret cannot stand without pain, support his weight normally, or move or walk normally, then it is possible that he may have a broken bone. A ferret with a broken limb may vocalize, cry, or

Immobilize your pet in a towel if you suspect he has a broken limb.

make some other unusual noise when picked up. There may be visible or internal swelling, with tenderness at the affected area. You should restrict the ferret's activity or immobilize him in a towel until veterinary attention can be sought.

Never attempt to wrap an injured leg or put a splint in place without help from someone with experience in caring for injured animals. You can do more harm than good. Keep the ferret immobilized and get him to a veterinarian quickly. If the bone is protruding from the skin, be sure to staunch any blood as carefully as possible, but don't attempt any heroic measures. Wrap and run!

Wounds and Cuts

If your ferrets have had a tussle among themselves or have gotten into a fight with another animal, superficial puncture wounds or cuts should be treated by applying hydrogen peroxide, then applying an antibacterial ointment. If the wound appears deep, if you can see bone or sinew, or if you cannot control the bleeding, a trip to the vet will be necessary.

Taking care of a puncture wound or cut doesn't stop with the initial treatment. It's important to keep a close eye on the area and watch for abscesses or infection. In severe cases, an abscess may have to be reopened by your veterinarian and allowed to drain.

Part 3

Infections or abscesses may need to be treated with a mild antibiotic.

Home Treatments

It's very important to contact a veterinarian or experienced ferret person when you first notice symptoms that you think might be health-threatening. No matter what anyone tells you, you should never attempt to treat your ferret yourself, especially if the illness is severe.

Never give your ferret aspirin or other pain relief medicine designed for humans. Aspirin is not a good enough pain reliever in emergency cases, and its effects in ferrets are totally unpredictable. As hard as it may be to watch your ferret writhing in pain, do not attempt to relieve his pain before a veterinarian sees him, as the pain symptoms may help your veterinarian in quickly diagnosing the problem. Masking the pain symptoms can result in misdiagnosis, which could be fatal. Some veterinarians may recommend anti-diarrhea medications for diarrhea, however, since most cases of diarrhea are simply the body recognizing a need to remove noxious agents out of the body quickly. However, most holistic and homeopathic veterinarians agree that unless the diarrhea is truly life threatening, it is perhaps best not to interfere with the process. Anti-diarrhea products should be used if diarrhea is profuse and dehydrating, possibly as a result of an enterotoxin or severe bacterial enteritis. You should always talk to your veterinarian before starting any anti-diarrhea medications.

How to Plan for an Emergency

Effectively handling emergencies is done more easily if you set the stage long before your pet is ever sick. Use the following as a guide to prepare for emergencies both before and after they occur in your ferret.

Think Ahead

Knowing ahead of time what you should do in the face of any emergency is critical in gaining a successful outcome. It will allow you to remain calm, which is imperative in these circumstances.

Have your plan set long before you notice that first cough, sneeze, or see a sign of blood. Should an emergency arise, you can act faster, and calmer, and your ferret will be in good medical hands in a fraction of the time it would take for you to frantically take care of last minute contingencies if you weren't so well prepared.

Dangerous Plants

The Animal Poison Control Center lists the following plants as poisonous to animals. There is an extensive list on their website of the symptoms of the poisoning of each, what part of the plant is considered poisonous, as well as a full description of each plant. If your ferret has ingested any of these plants, contact the Animal Poison Control Center or your veterinarian immediately.

Aloe	Elephant Ears	Oleander
Amaryllis	English Ivy	Onion
Asian Lily	Foxglove	Orange Day Lily
Avocado	Gladiolas	Peace Lily
Azalea	Golden Pothos (Devil's Ivy)	Philodendron Pertusum
Bird of Paradise	Heartleaf Philodendron	Poinsettia
Buckeye	Holly	Red Lily
Buddhist Pine	Horsehead Philodendron	Rhododendron
Caladium	Hyacinth	Saddle Leaf Philodendron
Calla Lily	Hydrangea	Sago Palm
Ceriman (Split or Cut Leaf Philodendron)	Iris	Satin Pothos
	Japanese Yew	Stargazer Lily
Charming Dieffenbachia	Lily of the Valley	Tiger Lily
	Macadamia Nut	Tomato Plant
Christmas Rose	Mauna Loa Peace Lily (Peace Lily)	Tree Philodendron
Clematis		Tulip
Corn (or Cornstalk Plant)	Mistletoe (American)	Variable Dieffenbachia
Daffodil	Morning Glory	Variegated Philodendron
Day Lily	Mother-in-Law	Wood Lily
Deadly Nightshade	Narcissus	Yew
Easter Lily	Nightshade	Yucca

The first thing you must plan is where you can take your ferret for emergency care. Sad to say, not all animal hospitals or emergency clinics will see ferrets. Because there are only a limited number of emergency clinics to begin with, finding a veterinarian to help a ferret owner during an emergency can be especially daunting.

Ferret-proof your home to prevent injuries or death.

Remember the Medications

Make yourself a note in your emergency kit to be sure to pack all of the ferret's current medications. Many daily medications can interact, sometimes fatally, with some emergency medications. The emergency room staff will need to know not only the drug, but also the current dosages being administered and the last time they were given.

The best way to establish an emergency plan is to ask your veterinarian for help. She can either suggest a suitable facility, or you can make arrangements with her ahead of time for her to provide after-hours care that might not be available otherwise. Remember, the time you take now could save your pet's life later.

Once you know where you are going to go, be sure you know how to get there. Go to a good mapping website and print out a map and directions from your house to the emergency veterinarian location. Be sure you write the phone number of both your regular vet and the emergency veterinarian on this map. It's hard enough to find a strange location under the best of circumstances, and trying to find a vet's office or clinic during a crisis can be overwhelming.

If you don't own a car (or don't drive), you should have the phone number of a taxi service in your area that transports pets, or the number of a friend or family member that will be willing to drop everything to play ambulance driver for your furry friend.

Be sure you have an up-to-date record from your regular veterinarian of all current vaccinations, past treatments, and past problems. Doing so can save you money if tests have been run and the results have been recorded. This can also eliminate the possibility of your ferret being overmedicated if you have current records showing all medications that have been administered recently.

An Ounce of Prevention

There will always be some problems and emergencies that will be out of your control. Many emergencies can be avoided by using the old adage that "an ounce of prevention is worth a pound of cure."

A lot of prevention measures can be taken simply by watching your ferret closely and realizing the potential problems that can stem from his specific temperament. If he is a chewer, be sure that all electrical cords and other potentially harmful "chew toys" are kept out of his reach. Does he leap blindly from heights? Watch your ferret carefully to make sure he isn't allowed to climb higher than he can withstand a fall. Does he put things that are small enough to swallow in his mouth? Is your ferret a Hairy Houdini? Check and double-check every possible escape route. Be especially cautious about recliners and rocking chairs—many ferrets have lost tails, limbs, and lives to these common hazards.

After determining where to go and how to get to the emergency hospital, it's important to know how you will transport your pet. Just tossing a towel around him and heading for the car is not a wise decision. A ferret in pain can move quickly and can cause a lot of damage in a short amount of time without meaning to do anything wrong. A secure pet carrier is a must, and it should be padded with clean towels or another soft blanket material.

Emergency Assessment

What constitutes a real emergency? You should have a plan in place for what do in case of one. You have thought of every conceivable injury or illness your ferret might suffer. But, at what point do you put that plan in effect? When do you admit that things are beyond the "vague concern" stage, and into emergency mode?

Sometimes vague symptoms can be the signal of something drastic and life threatening, or just a passing discomfort. For instance, the difference between just a stomachache and a gastrointestinal obstruction may be subtle on the outside, but are very different internally. If there is any doubt as to whether your ferret is in an emergency situation or not, consider it an emergency and take the necessary steps. It's much better to be safe than sorry.

Possible Emergencies

Sometimes symptoms of illness are more elusive, and an accurate evaluation of their severity will depend upon how well you know your pet. If your ferret usually goes insane over his daily raisin treat but tonight turned up his nose and wandered listlessly away, you

Sometimes a lethargic pet is tired from playing too much, not from illness.

True Emergencies

Some symptoms will always necessitate an immediate trip to the emergency room. These include:

·Non-responsiveness

·Difficulty breathing

·Severe acute pain

·Open wounds or active bleeding

·Unproductive urination

·Seizures or convulsions

Part 3

have to count on your own evaluation to decide the severity of the situation. That will include a reconstruction of the day's events. Did the ferret eat treats earlier, and perhaps just isn't hungry now? Did he refuse his breakfast earlier? Have you witnessed any other troubling symptoms (inability to urinate, lots of trips to the litter pan, excessive sleeping)? Has the ferret seemed as active as usual all day? Is he just tired from a rousing game of "chase the towel" around the room?

Help! My Ferret is Choking!

If you suspect that your ferret may be choking on a foreign object, you can use the Heimlich Maneuver. This forces air out of the lungs, which pushes the object out of the throat. If your ferret is choking, place the ferret on his side. Support the spine with one hand, and with the other hand, grasp the abdomen just below the ribcage. Gently press in and up with the hand positioned below the ribcage. Repeat until the object comes out or until the animal is transported to the veterinarian.

Note: Be careful not to use too much force because this could cause internal damage.

If there are no other troubling symptoms, try repeating the offer of a treat a little later, and see if you get the same response. If the ferret seems to be sleeping normally and is having regular bowel functions, you can probably wait until the next day and go to your regular vet for a checkup.

Don't bother calling an emergency clinic to see if they think your pet should be brought in. Their rule of thumb is, "If the owner thinks it's an emergency, then we have to treat it like an emergency." They would rather be safe than sorry with your pet, so they'll tell you to bring the ferret in for evaluation. Don't waste their time or yours by asking lots of questions. No matter how much information they are given, it's impossible for them to evaluate your pet over the telephone and tell you if the ferret is critically ill. Only a hands-on exam can do that. If you're in doubt, go.

Home Care

If you've evaluated your pet and decided that you're not looking at a real emergency, it's time to think about what kind of home first-aid you can offer your ferret to make him more comfortable. Unless you are a very experienced ferret owner, this is not a wise decision, and most veterinarians will not recommend any kind of home therapy until the ferret has been checked out by a professional. However, if you know your ferret well and are comfortable with your decision, there are some things you can do while waiting for your regular veterinarian to arrive at the office for her regular hours.

First Aid for a Weak Ferret

Try offering a small amount of pancake syrup orally. Give only drops at a time because a diminished swallow response could cause your ferret to drown. The theory here is that a weak ferret may have a very low blood glucose level; the sugar in the syrup can help to correct that.

First Aid for Bleeding

Apply direct pressure. Bleeding can cause significant problems in a short amount of time for anyone, especially if you only weigh two pounds. After holding pressure on the area for five minutes, release the pressure and evaluate. If the bleeding resumes, apply pressure again and call the clinic to tell them you're on your way with your ferret.

Disaster Emergency Tips

Not all emergencies can be expected or prevented. Some are acts of nature and these must be prepared for with your pets in mind as adequately as the health problems mentioned previously.

The Cost of Care

You should be aware that emergency care is expensive. While you can't put a price tag on a beloved family pet, if a trip to the emergency clinic can be avoided without creating a dangerous situation for your ferret, you should take that into consideration. Many emergency facilities will require payment in full when services are delivered or at least a significant deposit if the pet is admitted to the hospital. An emergency room trip can cost hundreds of dollars or more depending on the problem, what treatment is required, and whether your pet must be hospitalized for any length of time.

Part 3

Another ferret owner can evacuate your pet if you can't reach home in a natural disaster.

Pet Safety in Case of Emergency

Put a sticker in a window near the front door specifying location and number of animals in the house. This will alert rescue workers to the fact that even if humans don't answer the door, there are other "family members" that need assistance. Always keep a card in your wallet stating that you have animals at home that need to be taken care of. The card should also include the name of the person that should be notified if you are incapacitated, so he or she can take care of your ferrets.

If you live in an area that is prone to weather disasters, such as tornadoes, hurricanes, earthquakes, or flooding, you know that disaster can strike at any time. Natural disasters can be anything from a snowstorm that keeps you housebound for days without electricity or water, to an earthquake or forest fire that destroys homes.

Have you made preparations for your ferret's emergency care in these cases? What if you have to evacuate? Will your ferret have a safe shelter? It is important to put together an evacuation kit that stays beside the emergency first-aid kit at all times.

If you're in an earthquake-prone area, be sure that your ferret's cage is securely fastened in place and there are no large pieces of furniture nearby that could crush the cage if they fell. Have a small transport cage ready with a litter pan, food and water dishes, a bottle of water, and a bag with at least a three-day supply of food.

Always leave a trusted friend or neighbor with a key to your home so that someone else can take over the evacuation of your pets if you're away from home in an emergency.

Remember that the best way to avoid an emergency is to prepare for it. Use good safety practices. Be prepared, and be ready to roll if necessary to get your little buddy the best possible emergency care.

Ferret Behavior Problems

Anyone who owns a ferret will tell you that they can be wonderful pets. They're smart, charming, loving, sweet, funny, and clever. However, any ferret owner who is honest will also tell you that they can be devious, mischievous, and are certainly not a pet for everyone.

Although there are actually very few real temperament problems in most US-bred domesticated ferrets, some of the natural behaviors of a ferret are a little hard for some people to get used to. Living with a ferret is a bit like living with a two-year-old. He will throw temper tantrums when he doesn't get his way; he'll be able to think his way through problems (and into situations

Ferret owners view their pets as loving, sweet, charming, and mischievous.

Knowing why ferrets do what they do can help you modify their behaviors.

and possible trouble) you wouldn't have thought possible; he'll need constant care and supervision; and he'll always be convinced that the world revolves around him. But, while a human toddler will eventually outgrow the "terrible twos," a ferret is stuck in perpetual toddler-hood. Being a "ferret parent" means taking on the responsibility of working through the problems that will inevitably arise.

Knowing why ferrets do the things they do will give you insight on how to change the behaviors that are changeable and learn to deal more easily with, or possibly learn to accept, those behaviors that are simply inherent ferret genetic traits and, therefore, unchangeable. Any ferret, even the most peaceable and tractable, has the potential to become unruly and unmanageable very quickly and with little warning. However, if you take the time to really look at his world, you will usually find that something is amiss in your ferret's life. Whatever is making the ferret uncomfortable in some way is provoking the unusual behavior. This is something that you have the power to change if you will be patient enough to realize the problem and then work on solving it together.

Defining Bad Behavior

Most people would define "bad" behavior as behavior that causes problems between the ferret and the people (and other animals) that the ferret lives with. Unacceptable behaviors reported by a ferret owner could include the following:

√ Biting humans and other pets

√ Refusing to use the litter box

√ Harassing and fighting with cage mates

√ Digging holes in the carpet or being destructive when given free run of a room or the entire house

Think Like a Ferret

If your previously happy-go-lucky ferret suddenly starts exhibiting unacceptable behaviors, put yourself in his place for a bit. Think like a ferret, try to see the world through his eyes, and ask yourself the following questions.

- What is your housing like? Is it kept neat and clean or is it smelly and untidy?
- Do you get enough to eat?
- Are you provided with healthy foods that you like to eat?
- Do you get healthy treats and occasional surprises?
- Is your water supply kept clean?
- How often are you released from your cage to interact with your humans and animal friends?
- How are you punished when you do something wrong?
- How long has it been since you've visited your doctor for a checkup?
- Is your cage kept in a busy area of the house so you feel connected to other creatures even when you're confined?
- Do children or other pets in the house make you uncomfortable?

Looking at the world through a ferret's eyes may open your eyes to the causes of any behavior problems.

√ Refusing to eat his kibble and dumping it outside the cage

√ Looking for a way to escape from his protected area

√ Seemingly trying to attack his humans when he is turned loose.

Since we've established the fact that very few ferrets are "born bad," it becomes obvious that when a ferret suddenly displays behavior problems, the animal is either misunderstood, unhappy, or sick. Any one of those factors is

Adolescence

Just like humans and other mammals, ferrets go through a period of adolescence when everything is perceived as a potential plaything, a chew toy, or a mate. Hopefully your ferret is spayed or neutered, as this helps with problems of a sexual nature. If your ferret is descented, he or she was likely sterilized at the same time. If neither surgery has been done, they should be done as soon as possible after puberty (at around 6 to 9 months of age).

How you interact with your pet can affect his behavior.

sufficient to cause the relationship between a ferret and his owner to deteriorate. The good news is that almost any bad situation can be reversed, and the ferret's natural happy temperament can again surface so that a good relationship between the two of you can continue.

You may have to realize, however, that a behavior that seems "bad" or "wrong" to you may be completely natural to a ferret, even though it is annoying and unacceptable to a human. Many times, you must accept these typical ferret behaviors rather than attempt behavior modification. In fact, it may be your behavior that needs to be modified, not the ferret's.

Causes of Problems
Nature or Nurture?

It will be necessary to decide whether these behavior problems are "nature versus nurture." In rare circumstances, behavior problems are inherent in certain bloodlines, and thus will be harder to work through than behavior problems caused by human error in training, care, or neglect. However, problems that are genetic in nature are not insurmountable, and with the proper advice from a trainer or behavior modification specialist (or other knowledgeable "ferret person") and dedication on the part of the pet owner, these misbehaving ferrets can become valued members of the family.

Health Problems

It's wise to remember that behavior problems can also be symptoms of health issues. The first place you should take your new ferret is to the veterinarian for a complete checkup. Be sure that you've done your homework in choosing your vet and have found someone who has many other happy, healthy ferret clients. The vet will know what to look for to assure you that the ferret you've chosen should be around for a long time, given the proper care and treatment.

None of us stays healthy all the time. There will always be diseases, illnesses, and injuries to wreak havoc in our lives. It's the same with our pets. Ask your vet what symptoms you

Creature Comforts

Although a ferret appears to be closely related to a wild animal, it is completely domesticated to the point where he relies on his human for every aspect of his life, including the need to socialize. Your ferret will never be happy if he is left alone all day in a cage, even if the cage is enormous and filled with toys and treats. A ferret is very much the same as a young child. If you can imagine what a young child would do if he was left in a room alone, with nothing but a plate of food, water, and a few toys, then you can imagine why a ferret does the things he does when he's bored and lonely. Old or young, ferrets need at the minimum two hours per day to run loose in a closely supervised and protected area of your home, in close proximity of their family of humans and animal friends.

Pretty much all a ferret will ask for from life is to be allowed to run and play, to have toys that stretch his imagination, to bond with animal or human friends, to eat food he finds tasty, and to have plenty of time for nice, long, uninterrupted naps in a snuggly hammock in a clean cage. Provide him with these simple pleasures, and you may find that many of the "problem behaviors" you are currently experiencing will disappear.

should be on the lookout for, and always take your ferret to the vet if you notice any abnormal behavior in your pet. What you perceive as bad behavior may be a symptom of an illness.

An adrenal problem in ferrets is one very serious and possibly life-threatening health issue that can cause a normally well-behaved member of the family to turn into a terror. Caught early, even the more serious health issues can have a good prognosis, and hopefully your ferret will soon resume his normal, loving behavior patterns. Even non-serious health problems, as simple as teething in a young ferret or a bump or bruise on an older one, can cause a normally sweet and outgoing ferret to withdraw and become grumpy. Think about how you feel when you have a headache. You'd probably want to bite the hand that plucked you out of your warm cozy bed and demanded that you be entertaining.

Problems with Previously Owned Ferrets

It's never a good idea to choose a ferret that has been abused in a previous home unless you are a very experienced ferret owner. A ferret that has been abused or neglected in a previous situation is going to need a long period of adjustment and training before he can be trusted and before he will trust you. Where there is no trust, you can't be sure that the

Give your ferret a chance to show his true personality.

Individuality

Some behaviors are just peculiar to individual animals. After all, all humans don't have the same temperament or behave the same way in the same situations, so why should we expect anything different from our animal companions? Don't try so hard to make the perfect pet out of your ferret that you completely smother his individual character.

behavior patterns you're seeing are the ferret's true nature. He may be exhibiting certain behaviors just to get you to back off, or at the very least, to get a picture of him that may be nothing even close to his true personality.

Gaining this ferret's trust should be the first step you take before you attempt to modify any of his behaviors. It's always possible that once the ferret becomes comfortable in his new situation, the problem behavior that the ferret is exhibiting may disappear because that prior stimulus (the previous owner) is removed. Give your ferret a chance to show you his true personality before you begin any retraining or behavior modification practices.

The Adjustment Period

You should always give any ferret some careful scrutiny to be certain that what you're seeing is truly a "bad behavior" and is not just a misunderstanding on your part regarding his particular body language or the way the ferret was previously trained. It is also possible that his "bad behavior" (such as biting while playing) was considered acceptable or amusing by a previous owner, yet it might be something you cannot deal with, and will want to change as soon as possible. An adjustment period may be necessary before a firm schedule can be adapted for housetraining and behavior modification if your ferret is new to your household, no matter his age.

Disrupted Routines

Ferrets are creatures of routine. They will go to the bathroom where their litter box has been, even if the box is removed. Therefore, they will not do well with a family who constantly experiences life-altering changes such as moving. Ferrets enjoy a routine as long as it is fulfilling and contains enough variety (such as occasional new toys and bedding) to keep them entertained. If your family is constantly on the move or has a pattern of not following routines in other areas, make sure that the part of the world that involves your ferret changes as little as possible.

If you do move, make certain that the same furniture and rugs are in the room that the ferret has access to. Set up his cage in exactly the same way, in a similar location as in the previous house (facing a window, near a door, under a light fixture, where he can see the TV, or some other basic fixture that will be much the same in any house). Keep as much routine as possible and you'll have fewer problems with the way your ferret adjusts to the new situation.

Ferret Communication

If you have purchased a well-bred, healthy animal that has previously lived in a good situation with knowledgeable and caring ferret owners, more often than not the "unacceptable behavior" that the pet is exhibiting may be nothing more than retaliation for (real or imagined) slights, incorrect training, improper housing, or other treatment on the part of the previous owner. Quite simply, these are not problems, but are a breach of communication between the pet and the owner.

In the case of ferrets, sometimes the problems arise because the owner hasn't researched the species enough to realize that what they perceive as "abnormal" is simply a normal ferret, exhibiting normal ferret behavior. A ferret's actions that seem scary and unpredictable to an uneducated owner will be the very actions that a seasoned ferret

Try to learn your ferret's body language as much as possible.

Almost every movement a ferret makes means something.

owner will consider cute and endearing; oftentimes, the beauty of ferrets truly does lie in the eye of the beholder.

Most of the ferrets in animal shelters and with ferret rescue groups didn't end up there because their behavior problems were insurmountable. More often than not, the owner wasn't willing to take the time to get to know the ferret and try to understand what he was attempting to tell him through the only means of communication he has available: his sounds and actions. How much easier it would be to live with and train a ferret if he could talk. Since he can't, it's up to the dedicated owner to try to learn the ferret's language as well as possible.

As you get to know your ferret better, you will learn that his body language alone can tell you quite a bit about what he is feeling and what he wants. What can be perceived as aggressive behavior to someone who doesn't understand "Ferret-ese" will be understood by someone who reads ferret body talk as simply a barometer of the ferret's mood and does not necessarily indicate a bad temperament or behavior problem.

Ferret Body Language

Almost every movement that a ferret makes means something. It's definitely worth your while to spend some time learning ferret body language.

Hopping, Jumping and Bouncing Toward you

If your ferret jumps out at you from beneath the dust ruffle of your couch and grabs your ankles, he's playing, not really attacking you. People who are not familiar with ferrets sometimes think that the ferret is "after them." Indeed, sometimes it does appear as if he is almost lunging toward you in an aggressive action, but this is actually a ploy on the part of the ferret to engage you in play. If the ferret nips during that play, he's simply forgotten that you're not as tough as another ferret would be, and he just needs a gentle reminder that you're a tender-skinned human.

Part 3

Wild behavior

If your ferret dances (flings himself about on all fours with an arched back), clucks, races around careening into walls, furniture or people, bares his teeth, waggles his tail, or puffs his tail "bottle-brush" style, he hasn't really gone insane and he likely isn't angry with you—he's just being a ferret and engaging in some totally normal ferret hijinks.

If he chases you as you walk around the room, he's not really intent on doing bodily damage; he's just attempting to start a game of tag. Think of a kitten making the same moves, and you can easily see what's going on in your ferret's mind. Jumping toward him will instigate a game of chase and tag. If you're not in the mood for a game, simply sit or stand still and his attention will quickly move to a more interesting target.

Back Arched, Clucking

This is another game gesture. Again, think of a baby kitten arching its back, meowing loudly, as he sidesteps toward a littermate in a mock battle. Your ferret is simply talking to you and inviting you (or his cage mate) to join in some speedy ferret games. Getting down on his level and using your hand as a combatant for him (arching your hand, with your fingers on the floor and walking your fingers toward him, and then away from him) will keep him entertained for hours.

Running Backward

This will happen sometimes as you go to pick up your ferret. Although this may appear to be a fear gesture, it is most likely the same action a toddler might make when he's told it's time to stop playing and take a nap. Your ferret is not ready to go to bed (in his case, the cage) just yet, so he backs away from you, hoping to squeeze in a few extra moments of playtime (chasing him at this point would be sheer delight for him). To break this habit, pick up your ferret often while he is outside his cage for play time, give him a tasty treat, a quick caress, and then put him back down to play some more. This way, he does not always associate being picked up with being immediately put into the cage.

An arched back and clucking sounds are invitations to play.

Hissing and puffed-out hair are considered signs of fear.

In kits, wimpering denotes excitement.

Puffing out his Hair

When your ferret sits up tall on all four feet with his back slightly arched and all the hair on his body and tail standing on end, it's likely that something has either startled him, or he is the loser in a spat between himself and a battle partner. A ferret does this to make himself appear larger, and thus more formidable than he really is. This is also considered a fear gesture, often seen in ferrets that have been abused.

Putting Teeth on Your Hand While Being Held

Unless this is done in a nip action, putting his teeth on your hand is a ferret's way of asking (in his way of thinking at least) politely to be put down, or he could be warning you not to hurt him. Never jerk your hand away at this time, as this can cause an accidental injury to your hand (or in the case of a very young ferret, it could hurt the ferret's teeth). Use a training word such as "No," or "Careful," or "Stop!" as a warning that this action is unacceptable.

Continue holding the ferret for a few more minutes and perhaps give him a treat. Giving in to him and putting him down is a bad idea, as you'll be letting him know that the action scared you and will create a continuing problem as he learns to use his teeth to get his way. Be firm, but gentle in not giving into this action. Remember that you are dealing with a ferret here, not a Rottweiler. While a ferret's bite is certainly not fun, and it can draw blood, he won't do any lasting damage, and letting him have the last word (or tooth) in the matter can have a long-term detrimental effect to your relationship.

Biting

Very few ferrets actually bite with intent to do damage. A study of reported animal bites was conducted for a full year in New York City (the city that boasts the highest concentration of ferret owners, according to recent surveys of pet ownership). Results revealed over 1,000 cat bites, nearly 600 dog bites, over a 100 human bites and one (yes, only one) ferret bite.

It's interesting to note that although ferrets have such a bad reputation, they are the least likely of any of the pet species to inflict a serious bite. It's also notable that although a rabies vaccination only became approved for ferrets in 1990, there have been fewer than 25 cases of rabid ferrets since 1958. It's obvious that all along the line, good public relations for ferrets has been sadly lacking. It's up to you, as a responsible, loving ferret owner to help dispel these ill-founded and untrue rumors by making sure your pet is happy and content, well trained, well cared for, and is a good ambassador for the species.

Sound Language

Not only do ferrets have an extensive body language repertoire, but their sound language is fairly elaborate too. Don't worry if your ferret doesn't make much noise. Most of them don't. You'll quickly learn what your ferret is feeling by the sounds he makes, as well as his actions.

Clucking

This sound can range from a cluck or chuckle to what owners call a "dook dook" noise. Until you know your ferret well or you have an excellent understanding of ferret body language, it's sometimes hard to tell whether the ferret is very happy or very angry. Usually, however, clucking indicates happiness or excitement and is often uttered while playing or exploring a new area. This seems to be an "all-purpose" noise, and ferrets use it frequently to express a variety of emotions. It seems that when the noise is

A little time and effort can turn a misbehaving pet into an endearing family member.

associated with anger or fear, the noise seems to be a little more high-pitched and more rapid.

Whimpering/Whining

Young ferrets (kits) especially do this as a general excitement noise. It can also be uttered by the loser in a wrestling match.

Hissing

Hissing is more the sound of fear than aggression, although sometimes a ferret that is growing weary of unwanted attention from another ferret will use a hiss as a warning to back off.

Screaming, Screeching, or High-pitched "Chittering"

These sounds indicate extreme fright or pain. This is your cue that it's time to go rescue your ferret from whatever he's gotten himself into. It can also be a sign of extreme anger. A ferret that truly screams is in pain.

Although it is the nature of a ferret to be sweet, loving, and charming, sometimes those characteristics are overshadowed by those less desirable traits harkening back to their early roots. In that case, you must learn to handle each situation in the correct manner to create a bond of trust between the two of you. With just a little time and effort, you can turn even a misbehaving ferret into a charming and endearing member of the family.

Traveling with Your Ferret

It's vacation time! You've spent the last few weeks or months planning your vacation, your reservations are made, your clothes are packed, and suddenly it hits you that there is one family member that hasn't been considered: your ferret. Another major decision suddenly looms and questions need answers.

Could your vacation plans include your pet? Can your ferret handle being boarded at a boarding facility? Do you have a neighbor or friend who would enjoy having a houseguest, or would house-sit or pet-sit while you're gone?

If you have a friend or neighbor who would be willing to either take your ferret to his or her

You may have to take your pet on vacation with you

A ferret left home will likely be stressed at not having you around.

Pet Sitters

There are two major pet sitting organizations that can help you find a pet sitter in your area.

The National Association of Professional Pet Sitters

17000 Commerce Parkway

Suite C

Mt. Laurel, NJ 08054

Phone: (856) 439-0324

Fax: (856) 439-0525

Email: napps@ahint.com

Website: www.petsitters.org

Pet Sitters International

201 East King Street

King, NC 27021 (336) 983-9222

Fax: (336) 983-5266

Email: info@petsit.com

Website: www.petsit.com

home for the duration of your vacation, stay in your home to ferret-sit, or, as a last-case-scenario, come over daily to feed, water, and allow your ferret some free time, then the problem is solved. If that isn't an option, then you will either have to take your ferret on vacation with you or find a safe and pleasant place for him to be boarded while you're gone.

Pet Sitters

If you can't (or don't want to) bring your ferret with you on vacation, hiring a professional pet sitter to take care of him in his usual surroundings is a good alternative. Although the ferret will likely be stressed at not having you around, at least his surroundings will stay the same. Staying at home will eliminate the stress of being transported to a strange place, and the ferret will be able to remain in his familiar environment. Staying home will also eliminate the possibility of being exposed to other animals that might harbor unknown contagious medical problems.

Part 3

Boarding Facilities

Not all boarding facilities will accept ferrets, and few places will allow ferret owners to bring their own cages from home. However, most boarding facilities will allow a few of the ferret's toys and personal belongings (like a favorite shirt to cuddle with).

If you decide to board your ferret instead of hiring a pet sitter, you should keep in mind that many regular boarding facilities are not equipped for or knowledgeable about ferrets. They might agree to board your ferret, but you should take steps to be certain that you are leaving your pet in good hands. Asking a local ferret rescue group or ferret shelter workers for references or recommendations is always good idea. Many of them offer boarding services, especially to ferrets they have helped rehome. If they are not willing to keep your ferret, they can likely suggest someone in the area who is competent. Your veterinarian is another good contact for your search. Many times, if no one else in the area is willing to board ferrets, a vet's office will offer the service to their regular clients.

If all else fails, ask friends, relatives, and neighbors if they'd be willing to either pet-sit full-time in your home, take your ferret into their home, or as a very last resort, be willing to check on your ferret as often as possible, giving him the basic necessary care as well as some special attention time. Since this person may not be a "ferret person," be sure you leave detailed information about the necessary care, safety precautions, emergency (veterinary) information, and

Most boarding facilities allow a few of your pet's toys and belongings.

Sometimes friends and family agree to ferret-sit for a vacationing ferret owner.

Part 3

explicit contact instructions where you can be reached in case questions arise or if there is an emergency.

Whatever course of action you take, be certain that you have made your decision based on what is best for your ferret. Then, relax and enjoy your vacation knowing that he is well taken care of and as happy as possible.

Questions to Ask

There are many questions you should ask the staff of all boarding facilities before you make the decision to entrust your ferret to them.

√ Will your ferret be allowed outside of his cage during his stay? If so, how often?

√ Will people familiar with ferrets constantly supervise him?

√ Where will he be allowed to roam and how secure is the area?

√ Will he be allowed playtime with other ferrets?

√ What other species of animals do they board? Will your ferret be within hearing or smelling distance of them, or ever in direct contact with dogs, cats, etc.?

√ Can the boarding facility provide references from other ferret owners who use their services?

√ Do they have room for your ferret's cage or will they be supplying your ferret with one of their cages?

√ Do they mind if you bring items from home (cage, litter pan, snuggle sack, or toys) to make the transition less traumatic for your ferret if he will be required to stay in a different cage?

√ What shots are required for your ferret before his stay? Will all other ferrets he comes in contact with be vaccinated as well?

√ If the boarding facility is not in conjunction with a veterinarian's office, how do they handle medical emergencies? What veterinarian is on call for them? Is the vet familiar with ferrets? Would they be willing to use your regular veterinarian instead?

√ Do they charge extra for administering medicines or extra attention for elderly or ailing ferrets?

√ Will they call you at the first sign of any illness or undue stress from your ferret? (Be sure you provide adequate contact information before you leave, including a local contact person who is authorized to make decisions on your behalf.)

√ Do they provide food? What brand? If it's different from what your ferret is used to eating, will they feed his usual food if you provide it?

Get the answers to these questions before you finalize your plans to board your ferret. As always, if the conditions of the boarding facility aren't clean or if the staff seems uncooperative, leave and keep looking until you find a boarding facility that you feel comfortable with.

You should visit the boarding facility well in advance of the day you plan to leave your ferret at the facility. If possible, take your ferret along so he can be introduced to the sights, sounds, smells, and the people who will be providing his care. Offer him some special treats so the trip will be a pleasurable experience for him.

Make sure that the facility is clean, as quiet as possible, and that every effort is being employed to make the animals as happy as possible during their stay. There should be no overpowering scents or noises, and the employees should not be afraid to handle or play with your ferret. If any of

Have ferret, can travel with a Nylabone® Fold-Away Pet Carrier.

Part 3

the caregivers are afraid of your ferret or are repulsed by him, keep looking for a new boarding facility. Your ferret will not be comfortable around people who are not comfortable around him. Unless you can be assured that the people who will care for him on a daily basis truly care about his well-being, you will be happier continuing to look for the perfect place for him or consider making other arrangements entirely.

Taking Your Ferret with You

Taking your ferret with you is an option, especially if your vacation is a road trip. Although your ferret isn't going to be much help when it comes to watching for highway markers or helping to read the road map, he can be excellent company for you on long rides (so long as you remember to make an adequate number of stops with him).

Ferrets love to go places. You can fix up a carrying case with a litter pan and a space for food and water, and take him with you wherever ferrets are welcome. Most people suggest using a drip bottle in the cage for watering while on the road. This will keep the cage or travel crate dry and help to avoid spills. Make sure that your ferret doesn't get too hot or too cold on these trips out into the "big world."

Car trips don't seem to bother ferrets. In fact most ferrets will complain more loudly about being confined into a smaller travel cage than the actual movement of the automobile or the stopping and starting movements. Never let your ferret loose in the car because he can easily get beneath your feet while you're driving and cause an accident. Your fuzzy friend can also ferret his way through an undetected hole in the dash and climb into the engine compartment.

Tranquilizers

Tranquilizing your ferret for travel is not recommended unless the trip is absolutely necessary and your ferret has proven himself to not be a good travel candidate. Ask your vet about proper tranquilization practices and follow their instructions (and their warnings) to the letter. Never attempt to use other medications to make your pet drowsy. Remember, he may be unsupervised for several hours, and no one will be around to help him if he goes into distress.

Flying with Your Ferret

A few airlines will allow ferrets to be carried onto a plane in under-seat carriers as "carry-on luggage." Although most airlines will allow ferrets to be shipped in the cargo area, this isn't recommended. As careful as airlines try to be to ensure a pet's comfort during travel, there are hidden dangers such as extreme temperature fluctuations, loud noises (that can stress your ferret), and the danger of your ferret escaping from his cage and getting lost. However, cargo shipping can certainly be used in case of an emergency or during a move where not flying with your ferret would mean having to find a new home for him.

Be sure to get written approval if you plan on flying with your ferret. One person in the ticket office may say it's okay, but someone else on duty might say that ferrets are not accepted.

Staying in a Hotel

 If you're staying at a hotel or motel during your trip, be sure to notify the management (and housekeeping) that there will be a ferret in the room. Be prepared to pay a non-refundable deposit for the privilege of having your little furry travel partner along. It's a very good idea to take along a travel cage (some of them, such as the Nylabone® Fold-Away Pet Carrier, fold down into sizes not much larger than a suitcase) and promise to keep the ferret inside the cage when he's in the room, especially if he is alone. Even the most well-behaved ferret can have accidents when in a strange location or become overwhelmed by the various scents left behind by previous occupants, causing him to do damage to hotel property.

Keeping your ferret in a safe cage while you're not in the room will also help you avoid the worry of having a hotel or motel employee open the door without knowing that your ferret is loose inside, thus running the risk of having him escape into an area that is strange to both of you.

Remember that you and your ferret will be considered as representatives for every person who follows after you with his or her pet, so be on your best behavior. Don't allow your ferret to roam loose in the room unsupervised. Be honest and tell the management about any accidents or damage and offer to make restitution. You

Tell hotel management (and housekeeping) that there will be a ferret in your room.

Traveling With Your Ferret

You should bring the following items with you every time you travel with your ferret.

Proper paperwork: Always carry proof that your pet has been vaccinated for rabies. Most campgrounds and parks will not let you in without proof of shots and a valid rabies certificate.

Identification: Ferrets are likely to become very nervous in strange environments. Be sure your pet has on an ID tag in the unlikely event of his running away. This tag should have your name and a phone number where you can be reached while you're traveling. Leave a cell phone or beeper number, your vet's number, or the number of a neighbor who can forward any messages to you.

Food and water: Always carry a good supply of ferret food when you travel. Don't count on being able to find your normal brand in other parts of the country. Be sure the food is kept in a well-sealed container and feed your ferret a little less food than usual while you're traveling so as not to upset your ferret's stomach. Plenty of water is also very important, since stress can easily cause a ferret to become overheated when riding in a car, and he'll crave extra fluids.

Litter Pan: You should purchase a small litter pan that will fit into the ferret's travel cage. Make sure that the pan is securely fastened to the bottom of the cage. Be sure to bring an adequate supply of your ferret's litter along so you can change the litter while traveling.

Toys and Bedding: Take along some of your ferret's favorite toys and bedding that he had in his cage at home. They will make him feel more secure and help him realize that you are a common denominator in all situations in his life. Wherever you are, is home.

can't blame hotels and motels for refusing to welcome people traveling with their pets if they are continually met with undesirable "gifts" after pets have departed the premises. Just as none of us wants to step in dog waste when we take a walk around the motel grounds, the maid (or the next guest) will not be happy to find ferret "surprises" hidden in the closet or beneath the bed, nor will they be happy to discover chewed furniture, phone cords, or bedding. Make your ferret a model guest, and pave the way for those who follow you.

Ferrets and the Law

If you're going to be crossing state or country borders, make sure of what the law says in relation to ferrets before you arrive at a border crossing. Be prepared to have distemper and rabies vaccination proof in writing to show to border authorities. Know which states consider ferrets illegal, and which ones have the written authority to confiscate and/or put your ferret to death.

Why do some states have such stringent legislation? Most of these laws were passed because of the popular misconception that ferrets pose a serious rabies danger. Studies have indicated that it's hard for a ferret to catch rabies, and when one does, it dies very quickly, so the danger to others is very small. Another reason for banning ferrets is the idea that escaped pets will form feral packs and threaten livestock or native wildlife. There are no confirmed cases of feral ferrets in the US, and the few deliberate attempts to introduce domestic ferrets to the wild have failed miserably, so this, too, is an unfounded fear.

Lost Ferrets

Always keep your ferret closely confined when you're away from home. Having a lost ferret is terrible enough when you're on your home turf, but in strange surroundings it can create overwhelming

Know which states ban ferrets and have the authority to confiscate them.

Travel Tips

• Don't feed your ferret for two to three hours before you leave home. Feed him sparingly while you're on the road to avoid upsetting his stomach.

• Make sure your ferret can see out of his crate, and keep a window cracked open so he can get fresh air while he's in the car.

• Never leave any pet unattended in a vehicle, even if he is securely ensconced in his crate. This is especially important during warmer months when temperatures inside a car (even one with windows left partially opened) can quickly kill a pet.

• If you know you that will have to be away from the vehicle during your trip, leave your pet at home where he will be safe.

problems. Carry a photograph of your ferret with you in case your ferret gets lost and you have to create "Lost" posters. This photo can also be used as identification and proof of ownership if the ferret is turned in to a shelter.

Although a few lost ferrets are found and happily gathered back into the family fold, many others are not so lucky. Because few ferrets learn to come when they're called and because they're so good at hiding, they're virtually impossible

Part 3

An ID tag and a bell are travel essentials for ferrets.

to track down once they get into new territory outdoors. It's a very good idea to find something that your ferret will always come to, such as a favorite squeak toy, the rattle of a treat bag, or perhaps a special whistle you use only at feeding or treat time. Some people have trained their deaf ferrets to come to a flashing light, but obviously this isn't going to be of much use in broad daylight when your ferret has escaped.

Keep a lightweight collar on your ferret at all times during travel and make sure that your ferret wears an identification tag and a bell. The bell might help you find him, and the ID tag will help the finder contact you.

Part 3

Caring for the Older Ferret

Because ferrets have short life spans, old age sometimes seems to occur before you know it. Seemingly overnight, that bright-eyed little baby has become one of the elderly. Age brings with it a closeness and bonding that is not always easy with a young, more active ferret, as well as the inevitable changes and problems associated with being a senior citizen.

Feeding

One of the major changes you should make as your ferret matures is to change his diet accordingly. A mature ferret, upon reaching four years of age or so, may require less protein in his diet. Read the labels on ferret foods and choose

As your ferret becomes a senior citizen, his needs will change.

As your pet ages, change his diet accordingly.

General Behavior

Regardless of age, a ferret is a hyper-energetic little bundle of fur and is constantly getting into everything. You'll still be seeing the ferret doing his "dances" and keeping up with the youngsters. Sometimes it's hard to imagine that the ferret is getting older when he still plays like a kitten and doesn't seem to have a care in the world.

Usually, a geriatric ferret will sleep longer and sounder than a younger ferret might, so be sure he has an especially cozy spot in which to nap. You should respect the fact that older ferrets need more sleep and don't make him play (or allow children or other pets to bother him) when he doesn't want to be bothered. However, if you should notice an excessive or sudden change in your ferret's sleep habits that seem unusual, consult the vet as soon as possible.

one that has lower protein—most will be labeled "adult" instead of their regular formula. The lower protein is said to be easier on the ferret's kidneys. You should discuss this with your vet as your ferret ages. The changeover should be gradual by mixing the original formula with the "adult" formula over several days to avoid an upset stomach. Diarrhea in the geriatric ferret can be especially dangerous. Ferrets will usually easily convert their diet if you use the same brand of food and mix the old food in for a short while.

Your elderly ferret should still be eating about the same amount of food on a daily basis unless his energy level has dropped drastically. Such an energy drop might be the symptom of a medical condition, however, and the ferret should be examined by a vet as soon as possible to rule out more a serious problem.

Ferret Foot Care

The pads of the feet in older ferrets may become hard and dry and develop little growths. A small amount of Vitamin E cream or oil rubbed on the pads daily will help keep them soft and remove excess tissue.

Home Health Care

The ferret will go through several physical changes as he gets older. These changes are, for the most part, natural signs of aging and shouldn't pose many problems. However, contact your vet if you have questions about your ferret's behavior, physical appearance, or general well being.

The Coat

The older ferret's coat may become drier and more brittle as he ages. Don't bathe your ferret too frequently, as this will strip away the natural skin oils and worsen the condition. Bathe your pet as infrequently as possible, and no more than once a month (unless your veterinarian suggests you do otherwise), and use a gentle pet shampoo. You may also use special preparations such as emollient sprays to add moisture back to the skin after bathing or between baths. If you notice hair loss, skin changes, growths, or excessive scratching, have your ferret examined by a veterinarian to rule out any serious skin disorders.

Loss of Control

You may notice that your ferret has less control over his bladder and bowels as he ages. Always make sure that the litter box is easily available. Put out a few extras if your ferret roams around so he won't have too far to go to find a bathroom.

Senior ferrets may become weak in the hind legs for a variety of reasons, so you may have to make adaptations to the ferret's cage and litter boxes to make

Contact your vet if you have questions about your pet's appearance or well-being.

Hairballs can be treated with certain medications.

Part 3

them more accessible. Use ramps if necessary to help your ferret get in and out of the box. Any sudden or unusual weakness or loss of balance should be brought to your veterinarian's attention.

Hairballs

Use a cat hairball laxative at least once a week to prevent the formation of hairballs in the stomach. Brushing your pet regularly will also help to cut down on the amount of hair swallowed.

Expanded Veterinary Health Care

Ferrets start to show old age or geriatric problems after they are about three years of age. Therefore, starting a program of extra veterinary care at that time, as well as the special home care mentioned above, can extend the life of your pet and maintain his quality of life.

More frequent vet checkups are recommended for senior ferrets. Most veterinarians recommend that this be done every six months. Ferrets can develop illness and disease rapidly, especially the increasingly common cancers, and kidney and heart disease. Waiting an entire year between visits could prevent the early detection and management of these diseases.

Hair loss could indicate a number of conditions and should be treated by your vet.

Most vets prefer that some additional laboratory work be done starting at three years of age. On a healthy animal, it is recommended that a complete blood cell count (CBC) and fasting blood glucose be done. Don't feed your ferret for four to six hours before the tests are to be run. Your vet may also wish to do additional laboratory work, such as a blood chemistry profile and/or an X-ray for additional information, particularly if your pet is exhibiting signs of illness. Sedation may be necessary for the X-ray. Make certain that your vet uses isoflurane as the sedative of choice because it is much easier on the ferret's tender system.

After the age of seven, diagnostic testing may have to be done every six months along with a semiannual exam. These laboratory workups will be invaluable in detecting any disease early and thus facilitating treatment and prolonging your pet's life.

It's very important that you keep up with the annual canine distemper vaccination. Remember, distemper isn't just a "baby illness"–the older ferrets can contract distemper just as easily as the youngsters can.

A heartworm preventive should also be continued if your pet is kept outdoors or is taken outdoors frequently in the spring and summer.

Cancers

Unfortunately, neoplasia (cancer) is the most common cause of death in the older American ferret. In fact, well over 75 percent of all ferrets will develop some form of cancer in their lifetimes. The only way to combat cancer is with early detection and appropriate therapy. These are four of the most common types of cancer seen in the older ferret.

Lymphosarcoma

This cancer is not restricted to old ferrets, but it is seen more often in geriatrics. In many ferrets, it tends to go unnoticed with no symptoms for months or years, and then suddenly appears in a variety of forms. It is a cancer of the lymphatic system, which is part of the body's immune system. The cause is suspected to be a virus, although much is still unknown. The current theory is that the virus is initially transmitted from mother to kit, where it may lie dormant for a long period before causing a problem.

Signs of this cancer vary, and many animals have no outward signs for a long period of time. Changes that might be more noticeable may include: swollen lymph nodes, lethargy, frequent illnesses (such as "colds"), poor

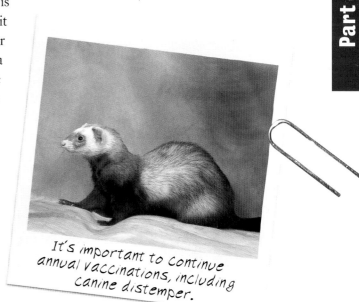

It's important to continue annual vaccinations, including canine distemper.

Your pet may seem to mellow as each birth-day passes.

appetite, difficulty breathing, chronic diarrhea, or hind limb weakness.

The diagnosis is made from a complete blood cell count and either a biopsy of a lymph node, a bone marrow biopsy, X-rays, or biopsies of other affected areas. Treatment is achieved through chemotherapy. Most ferrets tolerate the therapy very well and have few side effects, and most vets report about a 50 percent success rate with life being prolonged from six months to five years post treatment. Chemotherapy isn't always recommended. A quality life can still be possible for a period of time with only the judicious use of nutritional therapy and corticosteroids.

Insulinoma

Insulinoma is one of the most common cancers in the geriatric ferret. At least 50 percent or more of ferrets over three years of age will develop this disease. It is a cancer of the beta cells of the pancreas (the cells that produce insulin). This cancer causes these cells to produce abnormally high levels of insulin. This increase in insulin has the effect of driving the sugar out of the blood stream and into the body's cells at too rapid of a rate. This causes a dangerous decrease in the blood sugar level. The brain, which needs a constant large supply of sugar, then becomes sugar starved and begins behaving in an erratic manner. An abnormally functioning brain provides most of the warning signals. Early in the disease, the body counteracts the sugar drop by producing more sugar from the liver, which then temporarily corrects the problem, so symptoms are very subtle. As the disease progresses, and the body is less able to cope with the situation, the signs become more severe and last longer.

Early signs of the disease are usually no more noticeable than seeing the ferret staring blankly into space for a few seconds and then rapidly returning to normal. The ferret may be a little more difficult to awaken from naps. As the disease progresses, however, the signs

Part 3

become more specific and may include the following: drooling or salivating, pawing frantically at the mouth (all these signs are probably caused by a feeling of nausea when the sugar drops), extreme lethargy, seizures, coma, and death. The diagnosis of insulinoma is based on a fasting blood sugar level. The pet should be fasted for four to six hours. Occasionally it may also be necessary to run blood insulin levels at the same time.

Treatment depends on the stage of the disease when it is discovered, and the overall condition of the pet. Usually, surgery is the treatment of choice. If the tumor or tumors are removed, further medication may be unnecessary or at least can be delayed for some time. When surgery is not possible for whatever reason or in cases where the disease returns despite surgery, then medical management is indicated. This involves a good-quality, high-protein diet and the use of protein snacks, such as cooked meat and egg scraps, or strained meat baby food. The addition of brewer's yeast to the diet (in the amount of one-eighth to one-quarter teaspoon of powder two times daily with food) has also been helpful to stabilize glucose levels. Brewer's yeast contains chromium, which is known as the "glucose tolerance factor" because it helps to stabilize blood glucose and insulin swings. Absolutely no sugary treats should be given to the ferret, as this may make the problem worse. When diet no longer controls the signs, the ferret may have to be put on corticosteroids or an insulin-blocking agent. Treatment will be for the rest of his life.

If your ferret should experience any of the signs listed above, especially the serious ones such as seizures and coma, you can help bring him out of it by administering some honey and water by mouth until he is more alert or has stopped seizing. It should go without saying that you should contact your veterinarian and have your pet examined as soon as possible.

Adrenal Adenoma or Adenocarcinoma

This cancer is as common as insulinoma and frequently occurs along with it. This is a cancer of the adrenal glands (very tiny organs about the size of half a pea, located near the kidney). These glands produce very potent hormones that control a number of metabolic functions in the body. Ferrets may develop adenoma, which is the benign form of the disease (which means that it does not spread to other organs of the body) or adenocarcinoma, which is the malignant form. They may develop this disease in either one or both glands.

Part 3

Signs of this disease are fairly specific and are related to an overproduction of hormones, particularly abdrogens, the precursors to the sex hormones. The most common sign seen is a hair loss over a portion or all of the body. The hair loss may come and go over a period of time. In spayed females, the vulva may swell as if the female was in heat again. Other signs may include one or any combination of the following: intense itching, dry brittle hair, thin or red, scaly skin, weakened muscles, increase in body odor (as if the pet was not descented), anemia, and lethargy. The diagnosis is based primarily on the symptoms. However, if the diagnosis is questionable, your veterinarian may recommend submitting a blood sample to a lab for hormone level evaluation.

The treatment of choice is the surgical removal of the affected adrenal gland. Since the disease and insulinoma frequently occur at the same time, any insulinomas can also be removed.

Skin Tumors

Skin tumors in older ferrets should be surgically removed as soon as possible, not from an aesthetic point of view, but because of the possibility that some are malignant and can spread to other areas of the body. The most common type of skin tumor in the ferret is the mast cell tumor, which appears as a round, raised, button-like lesion. It may be quite itchy and often has a crust of dried blood over the top. It is usually benign but has been known to metastasize to internal organs, including the lungs.

Other common skin tumors are adenomas and adenocarcinomas. They are cancers of the skin glands and can occur anywhere. In males they occur frequently at the tip of the prepuce and appear as a bluish-colored lump. Adenocarcinomas are highly malignant and should be removed as soon as possible. Your vet can determine the difference in non-harmful skin growths and lesions and those which could cause severe health threats.

Time to Say Goodbye

As much as you enjoyed your ferret's companionship during his childhood and teenage years, you'll find you become even more attached during his geriatric years. Although an older ferret requires more constant supervision to keep him away from drafts or to keep his temperature regulated (ferrets are more sensitive to temperatures, as are older people), you will notice that your pet will seem to "mellow" as each birthday passes. He may want to spend more time just sitting on your lap instead of looking for trouble. He may be just as active as ever during playtime, but the playtime may be decreasing in length with each passing year.

No matter how well you have cared for your elderly ferret, or how much you love him, it will eventually come time to say goodbye. Death is a natural part of life, no matter how painful we find the prospect. Ferrets ask for nothing more than your love, company, and consideration during their last hours.

While many ferrets simply fade away peacefully when their time comes, others may rely on you to make the final decision for them. Discuss your ferret's overall health situation with your vet, and ask for help in deciding when it is time to let go. As long as your ferret is comfortable, is not in any pain, and is eating and eliminating with no problems, you can keep him with you for many years to come.

Properly caring for an aging ferret takes a large commitment of both time and money. The decision to euthanize a terminally ill ferret is made even harder on the owner because old or sick ferrets often seem aware of their increased dependence on their owners and become more responsive and affectionate. When your ferret's quality of life diminishes to the point that he is in pain or discomfort and is not enjoying simple pleasures any more, it may be time to say goodbye.

Although ferrets in this country are plagued with a variety of illnesses as they get older, they are very lucky to be living in this day and age, when frequent examinations and laboratory testing can greatly improve their chances of survival and prolong their lives. Continue to give your older ferret love along with special attention, and he will reward you with endless hours of laughter and affection throughout his silver years, into the golden years, and beyond.

Your pet will give you hours of laughter into his golden years.

Part 3

Ferret Rescue Organizations

To someone unaccustomed to the terms used in the animal world, the term "ferret rescue" possibly brings to mind a red truck with lights flashing, on its way to pluck a hapless ferret from harm's way. While there is no red truck or flashing lights, people who do ferret rescue on a daily basis are "angels of mercy" much like the paramedics, firefighters, and other professionals who provide human rescue in emergency situations. In this case, however, "rescue" refers to the taking in of a homeless animal that would otherwise turn up in a shelter or pound, in yet another bad home situation, or even worse, turned loose on the streets.

If you are considering purchasing a ferret, visit

Volunteers help find homes for homeless or abandoned ferrets.

your local animal shelter first. Adopting a ferret from a shelter is a terrific way to do a good deed, and it is a benefit to you as well. A ferret shelter in a larger city will most likely have a wide assortment of colors and age groups to choose from, and the staff will be willing to help you decide which ferret would be the best choice for you and your family.

Shelter Volunteers

Volunteering to do animal rescue of any kind takes a great deal of dedication, as well as a lot of patience, love, and money. To do ferret rescue takes even more time, effort, and patience than it does to rescue other species. A ferret that has been

Shelter Wish List

Consider giving a donation or volunteering your services at one of your local ferret shelters. Many times, ferret shelters are run by individuals or families who pay all the necessary costs to care for the ferrets. Often, there are volunteers working there 24 hours a day, 7 days a week to care for the ferrets. A small financial donation or a single bag of ferret food can help feed several ferrets for a week. You can even purchase the ferret food online and ship it directly to the shelter if you choose to support a shelter that is outside your immediate area.

Most shelters are also in need of old blankets, towels, food dishes, and toys to help keep the ferrets comfortable. By volunteering your time, donating supplies, or giving the shelter money, you not only get a tax deduction (many shelters are registered as non-profit organizations) but you are also helping to make a lonely or sick ferret's day a lot brighter.

abused is extremely hard to deal with. It takes a good deal of patience to transform him into a trusting and loving pet that can be successfully adopted into a permanent home. Most ferret rescuers offer their homes on a permanent basis to any ferret that cannot be rehabilitated well enough to be a suitable pet for another home.

People who are dedicated to ferret rescue have probably "seen it all" in their quest to find shelter and permanent homes for homeless ferrets across the country. They probably have

Adopting a ferret from a shelter is a terrific way to get a new pet.

seen ferrets that have been so mercilessly abused that there is no hope for restoring their health or erasing their emotional scars. Volunteers have helped find new, loving, permanent homes for ferrets that were left homeless through the death or illness of the owner. Ferret rescue workers have heard every excuse as to why a ferret owner no longer wants his or her ferret. Some reasons are legitimate (such as someone suffers from allergies or the family is moving to a state that doesn't allow ferrets), but some people abandon their ferrets when the novelty wears off. No matter what the reason or circumstances behind the homeless ferret's arrival at the shelter, the volunteers do what they can to give him a safe and loving environment.

Not only are there many thousands of individuals volunteering to take in unwanted ferrets, but there are also many shelters across the country that were created specifically for ferrets. These shelters are maintained as a place for lost, sick, neglected, and unwanted ferrets to receive love from someone who understands them, to have companionship with other ferrets, and to hopefully find a new home. These shelters are wonderful resources for information about ferrets, ferret laws, ferret care, and possibly even the place you will find the ferret that will steal his way into your heart and home. Many ferret shelters will also board ferrets for their owners in cases of emergency, or if there are no other boarding facilities in the area. The money paid them for this care will go toward caring for the other ferrets entrusted to them.

Ferrets need owners who can deal with their unique needs and personalities.

Common Mandates for Rescue Groups

• To provide care for any and all unwanted, abandoned, and/or abused ferrets.

• To rehabilitate abused, injured or ill ferrets.

• To find suitable, permanent homes for all ferrets that are mentally and physically healthy enough to be adopted into new families.

• To provide a permanent safe and healthy environment for the ferrets that cannot be rehabilitated to the point to be able to exist in a family environment.

Part 3

S.O.S.–Support Our Shelters

Ferret shelters around the country are overcrowded and straining at the seams. The situation is bad and it's getting worse. The operators of ferret shelters give their time and money every day, often sacrificing their own needs to provide food, shelter, veterinary care, and love to thousands of ferrets who have been lost, abused, or simply dumped off by people who can't be bothered to follow through on their commitment to their ferret.

Support Our Shelters (S.O.S.) is a non-profit organization that aids needy ferret shelters. Through their website and Ferret Mailing List, they distribute the FML Shelter List which provides the name, address, and veterinary information for shelters all over the world with their current status in terms of bills, number of ferrets, etc.

Most of the funds S.O.S. raises go into a general pool for periodic distribution to the shelters on the list. Support is provided in the form of payment to their vets or gift certificates for ferret supplies. S.O.S. also administers donations designated for a specific shelter or specific emergency rescues of large numbers of ferrets.

Support Our Shelters hopes that you will join them by becoming involved with a shelter near you. You can find one on the shelter list on their website.

For more information contact:

Support Our Shelters

C/O Judith White
1236 Belfield Avenue
Drexel Hill, PA 19026-4211
Phone: (610) 446-8036
Website: http://SupportOurShelters.org

Email: Judith@supportourshelters.org

Why Are so Many Ferrets Homeless?

Although ferrets have gotten a bad reputation as being unruly, nippy little creatures, ferret behavior problems are not the number one reason for the overwhelming number of unwanted ferrets. Believe it or not, the ferret owner is often the problem. In most cases, the problems were caused by an uneducated owner who did not research ferrets before bringing one home. The new owner was most likely unaware of a ferret's true nature and needs, and made a snap decision to adopt a ferret.

Once the novelty of owning a ferret wears off and this owner is faced with a true responsibility, the situation sometimes rapidly declines to the point that the ferret has been neglected and abused. Often, emotional, physical, or behavioral rehabilitation must be given by the shelter or rescue people before the ferret can happily exist within a new home situation.

Other Causes

Many times a ferret owner won't want to pay the nominal fee charged by most shelter or rescue groups to take in an unwanted ferret, so they try to find him a home by themselves. This is why you may see so many "Free Ferret" or "Cheap to a good home" advertisements in your local newspaper. While some of these ferrets may be excellent deals, and many will come with a cage and all the necessary supplies, many times you could be just buying someone else's problem ferret.

If you decide to purchase a ferret through a newspaper ad, make sure that you spend an adequate amount of time with the ferret that you are considering adopting. See how the ferret has been treated and see how he responds to your affection. If you are shown a ferret that has behavior problems as a result of being neglected or mistreated, don't be tempted to "rescue" it yourself, but suggest that the owner contact the local ferret shelter or rescue organization who will be better equipped to rehabilitate and rehome this ferret.

Education is Key

Not only do ferret rescue organizations or shelters offer a port in a storm to ferrets in need, but they are also excellent resources for educating the public on the

Shelter or rescue staff often must rehabilitate abused ferrets.

Rescue volunteers promote the ferret as a safe, dependable house pet.

Part 3

special needs of ferrets. They don't try to tell anyone that ferrets are the pet for everyone, but instead try to help each person decide if they indeed are a likely candidate for "planned ferrethood."

Besides opening their hearts and homes to needy ferrets, most rescue volunteers make themselves available to do talks, seminars, and programs on general ferret care, training for behavior problems, and promoting the ferret as a safe, dependable house pet.

Be sure you've done your homework before you apply to adopt a ferret from a responsible shelter. These people want to make absolutely certain that this ferret, who has likely gone through a great deal of trauma in his short lifetime, is getting a home with someone who not only understands ferrets, but is also willing to make the sacrifices necessary to be a good ferret parent.

Are you the right human to adopt a long-waiting ferret?

Application for Adoption

Don't be insulted if you contact a shelter or rescue organization about adopting a ferret and are given a lengthy application to fill out. This application will likely ask you a lot of questions such as:

- What food do you plan to feed—and why?
- Do you know what vaccinations are necessary for ferrets?
- How will you choose a veterinarian?
- What kind of cage and accessories will you provide for your ferret?
- Where will this cage be placed?
- How many hours a day will your ferret be inside its cage?
- What kind of toys do you think are suitable for a ferret?

For information about a rescue group near You, contact:

STAR*Ferrets (Shelters That Adopt and Rescue Ferrets)

PO Box 1714

Springfield, VA 22151-0714

Website:
www.thepetproject.com/pam/starferrets.html

Email: starferrets@starpower.net

Get Involved

Ferret shelters and the people who run them can be fabulous sources of information about ferrets, both before your purchase and after. If you contact a ferret rescue organization before you purchase your ferret, you may discover that they have a ferret available for adoption that has been waiting for the right human to come along and take him home.

Do what you can to keep in touch with your area ferret shelter. Be willing to do your part to help those less fortunate ferrets, help those who donate so much of their time and of themselves to further ferret education, and offer hope and love to ferrets who might not have a chance otherwise. Making a donation of your time, money, or supplies will make your heart lighter to know that you have helped ease the pain of a fellow creature.

Ways to Help

If you'd like to help with ferret rescue, but can't actually open your home to foster ferrets, there are many other ways you can show your appreciation for the hard work done by rescue workers and help them help abandoned and mistreated ferrets. Almost all shelters have the same "want list" of supplies. Consider donating the following to a ferret rescue organization:

·Litter

·Litter pans

·Blankets, sleep sacks, hammocks, and other bedding

·Toys

·Food

·Gift certificates to ferret veterinarians

·Laundry detergent

·Cleaning supplies

·Money (Every dollar helps. If every person reading this book donated one dollar to a ferret rescue organization, the financial load would be lightened.)

Publications

Ferret Digest Magazine

Legion of Superferrets National

Rose Smith

PO Box 866

Levittown, PA 19058-0866

Email: losnational@earthlink.net

Website: http://home.earthlink.net/~losnational/

Modern Ferret Magazine

PO Box 1007

Smithtown, NY 11787

Phone: (631) 981-3574

Fax: (631) 981-3710

Email: modferret@aol.com

Website: www.modernferretstore.com

Books

Field, Mary

The Guide to Owning a Ferret

New Jersey: TFH Publications, Inc., 1998.

Website: www.tfh.com

Land, Bobbye

Your Outta Control Ferret:

How to Turn Your Frisky Ferret into a Perfect Pet

New Jersey: TFH Publications, Inc., 2003.

Website: www.tfh.com

Modern Ferret Magazine

The Wit and Wisdom of the Modern Ferrets:

A Ferret's Perspective on Ferret Care

Edited by Mary Shefferman, 2000.

Website: www.modernferretstore.com

Organizations

American Ferret Association, Inc.

PMB 255

626-C Admiral Drive

Annapolis, MD 21401

Phone: (888) FERRET-1

Fax: (516) 908-5215

Email: afa@ferret.org

Website: www.ferret.org

Newsletter: American Ferret Report

California Domestic Ferret Association (CDFA)

Hildy Langewis, membership director

PO Box 21040

Castro Valley, CA 94576

Phone/fax: (510) 886-4210

Email: cdfa@cdfa.com

Newsletter: Ferret Focus

Californians for Ferret Legalization

410 Mountain Home Road

Woodside, CA 94062

Phone: (650) 851-3750

Email: ferretsnews@aol.com

Website: www.ferretnews.org

Ferret Adoption, Information, and Rescue

Mary K. Van Dahm

PO Box 952

Westmont, IL 60559

Phone: (708) 681-3181

Fax: (708) 681-3198

Newsletter: F.A.I.R Report

Ferrets Anonymous

Pat Wright, chairman

PO Box 6497

Torrance, CA 90504

Phone: (626) 358-6027

Email: FAmail@ferretsanonymous.com

Website: www.ferretsanonymous.com

Newsletter: The Ferret Paw Print

Ferret Association of Connecticut, Inc. (FACT)

Ann Gruden

14 Sherbrooke Avenue

Hartford, CT 06106

Phone/fax: (860) 247-1275

Email: agruden@ferret-fact.org

Website: http://ferret-fact.org

Newsletter: Paw Printz

Ferret Family Services

Troy Lynn Eckart

PO Box 186

Manhattan, KS 66505-0186

Phone: (913) 456-8337

Fax: (913) 532-6315

Email: sprite@ksu.edu

Website: www-personal.ksu.edu/~sprite

Newsletter: Ferret News

Ferret Fanciers of Greater Milwaukee

Judy Vowell, shelter coordinator

PO Box 11625

Milwaukee, WI 53211-0625

Phone: (414) 464-3346

Email: ferret_otter@yahoo.com

Website: www.ffgm.org

Newsletter: Ferretorials

Ferret Friends

Ginny Childs, President

1067 W. Miracle Mile #4

Tuscon, AZ 85705

Phone: (520) 407-2063

Website: http://members.tripod.com/FerretFriends

Newsletter: Ferret Friends Newsletter

Ferret Services of Freedom

Stephanie Mudgett

6 Mudgett Drive

Freedom, NH 03836

Email: ferret.svcs@rscs.net

Website: www.ferretservices.com

Newsletter: The Shelter Scoop

Ferret Wise Rescue and Rehabilitation Shelter

Dino and Alicia Drakiotes

PO Box 561

Malborough, NH 03455-0561

Phone: (603) 876-4975

Email: ferretwise@top.monad.net

Website: www.ferretwise.org

Greater Chicago Ferret Association

PO Box 7093

Westchester, IL 60154-7093

Phone: (708) 442-8650

Website: www.gcfa.com

Newsletter: Off the Paw

Star*Ferrets

Pamela Troutman, director

PO Box 1832

Springfield, VA 22151-0832

Phone: (703) 354-5073

Email: starferrets@starpower.net

Website: www.thepetproject.com/pam/starferrets.html

Western NY & Finger Lakes Ferret Association (WNYFLFA)

Sharon Pease

PO Box 10085

Rochester, NY 14610-0085

Phone: (585) 482-9307

Email: wnyflfa@frontiernet.net

Website: www.wnyflfa.isfabulous.com

Newsletter: Ferret Chatter

Web Resources

Ferrets Across America

Website: www.geocities.com/imweeze

Ferret Central

You can find information about ferret shelters, clubs, vets, breeders, and products at this network to assist people who work with ferrets.

Website: www.ferretcentral.org

The Ferret Clinic

You can find clearly arranged information and articles about ferret diseases on this website.

Website: www.ferretnews.org/clinic.html

The International Ferret Congress

This site showcases sponsored events and symposiums for ferret owners, shelter operators, veterinarians, and breeders to learn the latest in ferret husbandry and sharing a love of ferrets.

Website: www.ferretcongress.org

Pet Finders

Petfinder.com

This is an online, searchable database of over 100,000 animals that need homes from over 5,000 animal shelters and adoption organizations across the USA and Canada.

Websites: www.petfinder.org, www.petfinder.com

Totally Ferret

At the Totally Ferret website, you can find information about nutrition and high-quality food for your ferret.

Website: www.totallyferret.com

Rescue and Adoption Organizations

The American Society for the Prevention of Cruelty to Animals (ASPCA)

424 East 92nd Street

New York, NY 10128-6801

Phone: (212) 876-7700

Email: information@aspca.org

Website: www.aspca.org

Animal Protection Institute

1122 S Street

Sacramento, CA 95814 or

PO Box 22505

Sacramento, CA 95822

Phone: (916) 447-3085

Fax: (916) 447-3070

Email: info@api4animals.org

Website: api4animals.org

Ferret Rescue Of Spokane

Tracy Kilmer, Director

1 W. Montgomery Road

Deer Park, WA 99006

Phone: (509) 262-9556

Email: ferretFROS@aol.com

Website: www.ferretrescueofspokane.org

The Humane Society of the United States (HSUS)

Companion Animals Section

2100 L Street, NJ

Washington DC 20037

Phone: (202) 452-1100

Website: www.hsus.org

Midwest Ferret Fellowship

Dee Gage & Joyce Palmiter

510 W. Howe Avenue

Lansing, MI 48906

Phone: (517) 267-0748

Email: Trofeo91@aol.com

Website: www.midwestferretfellowship.org

New England Ferret Foster, Education, and Rescue, Inc.

(NEFFER)

PO Box 1165

Westfield, MA 01086-1165

Phone: (413) 433-3863

Email: neferrets@neferrets.org

Website: http://www.neferrets.org

Pet Sitting Services

The National Association of Professional Pet Sitters

17000 Commerce Parkway

Suite C

Mt. Laurel, NJ 08054

Phone: (856) 439-0324

Fax: (856) 439-0525

Email: napps@ahint.com

Pet Sitters International

201 East King Street

King, NC 27021

Phone: (336) 983-9222

Fax: (336) 983-5266

Email: info@petsit.com

Website: www.petsit.com

Veterinary Resources

The American Veterinary Medical Association

1931 North Meacham Road, Suite 100

Schaumburg, IL 60173

Phone: (847) 925-8070

Fax: (847) 925-1329

Email: avmainfo@avma.org

Website: www.avma.org

Emergency Services

ASPCA National Animal Poison Control Center

1-888-426-4435

Website: www.aspca.org

Animal Poison Hotline

(888) 232-8870

Organizations

Index

A

Abdrogens, 186

Adenocarcinoma, 185

Adenocarcinomas, 186

Adenomas, 186

Adjustment period, 162

Adolescence, 159

Adoption, 35, 194

Adrenal Adenoma, 185

Adrenal disease, 135

Adult, 51

Adults, 50

Age, 35, 50

Aging, 181, 187

    Coat, 185

    Hairballs, 182

    Loss of control, 181

Ailments, 133

Albino, 47

Aleutian Disease, 136

Allergies, 139

American Ferret Association (AFA), 32, 47

Anal area, 45

Anal prolapse, 138

Anemia, 186

Aplastic anemia, 46

B

Back arched, 165

Badger, 49

Ban, 21

Bath, 25, 122-123

Bathing, 119-120

Bedding, 23-26, 33-34, 114, 59, 62-63, 82, 88-89, 94-95, 121,163,176

Bedding–corn-cob, 89

Behavior modification, 160, 162

Behavior, 15, 25, 27-28, 31, 45, 47, 52, 59, 72-73, 82, 111, 139-140, 157-164

    abnormal, 163

    aggressive, 164

    general, 180

    puffing out hair, 166

    putting teeth on owner's hand, 166

    wild, 165

Behaviors, 82, 82, 158-160, 162

Bib, 49

Biting, 14, 82, 139, 158, 162, 167

Black-eyed white pattern, 48

Black-eyed white striped, 48

Black-Footed, 12

Blanket, 24

Blaze, 47, 49

Boarding facilities, 171

Body language, 162, 164, 167

Body temperature, 43, 120

Bouncing, 166

Breeder, 32-34, 46, 56

Breeders, 17, 19, 31-32, 46, 107

Broken Bones, 149

Burrowing, 14

C

Cage, 16, 17, 23, 24, 25, 28, 33, 36, 38, 45, 58, 59, 60, 64,
 67, 68, 74, 85, 86, 87, 88, 90, 91, 93, 94, 112, 123, 141,
 159, 161, 163, 172, 175
 accessories, 89
 cleaning, 93
 placement, 91
 safety, 91

Cancers, 183-184

Canine distemper, 136
 incubation period, 138
 symptoms, 137
 vaccinations, 136

Cardiac disease, 138

Carnivores, 12

Carpet, 95

Cedar chips, 62

Cedar, 113

Champagne, 48

Chewer, 153

Children, 26, 29, 33, 72, 159

Chittering, 168

Chocolate, 48

Choking, 154

Cinnamon, 46, 48

Clucking, 165, 167

Cold, 81

Colds, 183

Colorations, 46

Commitment factor, 20

Communication, 163

Competition, 32

Convulsions, 154

Corticosteroids, 185

Cuts, 149

D

Dangers, 68

Deaf, 178

Deafness, 47

Declawing, 124

Dehydration, 148

Descented, 24, 33, 34, 37, 51, 161

Diarrhea, 109, 134-135, 137, 150, 180, 184

Diet, 67, 97-98,100, 102, 107, 179, 185

Digging, 82, 158

Disaster emergency, 155

Disease, 140

Diseases, 134, 160

Distemper, 132-133, 183

Domesticated, 12

Drooling, 185

Duck soup, 104-105

E

Ear, 125

Ears, 44

Emergency assessment, 153

Epizootic catarrhal enteritis, 134

Estrus, 46

Euthanasia, 137

Eyes, 43, 137

F

Fear gesture, 166

Feeding time, 100

Feeding, 179

Ferret laws, 191

Ferret rescue, 189-190, 193

Ferret shelter, 190

Ferret websites, 19

Ferret-ese, 164

Ferret-proofing, 63-64, 87

Fighting, 158

Financial issues, 25

Fine Points, 48

First aid, 155

    bleeding, 155

    weak ferret, 155

Flea shampoo, 120

Fleas, 142

Food, 22, 23, 25, 26, 51, 59, 60, 114, 125,156, 176, 195

Foods, 101, 108

    unhealthy, 102

Foot care, 180

Free-range, 86

Free-roaming, 85-86

Fungal infections, 126

Fur, 44

G

Gastric ulcers, 138

Gastrointestinal obstruction, 153

Gastrointestinal tract, 134

Gates, 66

Genetics, 47

Geriatric problems, 182

Gestation, 43

Gibs, 45

Green slime disease, 134

Grooming, 119, 125

    excessive, 139

H

Hairballs, 134

Hammocks, 23, 39, 59, 63, 81, 89

Handling, 75, 77

Harassing, 160

Hazards, 66

Head cold, 146

Health, 22, 34, 35, 37-39, 41-42, 57, 66, 93, 132-133, 140, 160-161

Heart disease, 138

Heart rate, 43, 147-148

Heartworms, 139, 143

Heat distress, 140-141

Heat stress, 93

Heatstroke, 141

Heimlich Maneuver, 155

Hiding, 14, 82

Hindquarters, 82

Hissing, 170

History, 13

Hobs, 45

Home care, 155

Home health care, 181

Hopping, 166

Household hazards, 63

Housing, 21, 159

Hunting, 14, 79

Hypoglycemia, 135

I

Illegal, 12

Immune system, 140

IMRAB-3, 132

Individuality, 164

Influenza, 139

Insulinoma, 135, 184-185

Intestinal blockages, 78, 123, 134

Intestinal disorders, 134

J

Jills, 45

Jumping, 164

K

Kidney disease, 138

Kit, 52, 57

Kits, 50, 137

Knee pads, 49

Knee patches, 49

L

Law, 178

Legality, 21

Lethargy, 134, 137, 139, 183, 185-186

Lifespan, 16, 43

Litter box, 158, 163

    habits, 112

    training, 116-117

Litter, 23, 24, 28, 34, 37, 38, 59, 61, 62, 82, 86, 88-89,94-95,111-113, 114-118, 154, 156, 195

Lost, 177

Lymphosarcoma, 136, 183

M

Mammal, 12

Mast cell tumors, 136

Misconceptions, 80

Mitt, 49

Multiple-species home, 26

Mustelidae, 12

N

Nails, 44

National Association of Professional Pet Sitters, The, 170

Nature versus nurture, 162

Neutering, 45-46, 51

Newspaper pellets, 62

Nipping, 28

Noise, 73

Non-descented, 24

Nose, 44, 137, 139-140

Nutrition, 97-98, 101, 106

    baby food, 106, 108

    vitamin supplements, 107

Nutritional requirements, 109

Nylabone® Fold-Away Pet Carrier, 90, 175

O

Obesity, 104

Odor, 23-24, 33, 39, 44, 45, 93, 95, 102, 119-121, 125

Ownership, 11, 15, 16, 21

P

Panda, 50

Pandas, 47

Panleukopenia, 137

Parasites, 142

Patience, 73

Patterns, 48

Paw pads, 137

Pawing, 187

Personality, 52

Pet Sitters International, 170

Pet sitters, 170

Phenols, 62

Point/Siamese, 49

Polecat,12-13

Presents, 67

Previously owned, 161

Problem behaviors, 161

Puberty, 159

Pulse, 147

Q

Quarantine, 77, 143

R

Rabies certificate, 176

Rabies, 57,132, 177

Recliners, 65

Rehabilitating, 51

Rescue groups, 166

Rescue shelters, 17

Rescue, 21, 31-32, 35-36, 189, 194

Respiratory problems, 113

Respiratory rate, 148

Roan, 49

Rodent control, 14

Running backward, 165

S

Sable, 46-47

Safety collar, 86

Salivating, 185

Scent glands, 24

Screaming, 168

Screeching, 168

Scruffing, 76

Seizure, 82

Seizures, 154

Sexual maturity, 43

Shock, 148-149

Skin tumors, 186

Sleep sack, 24, 81

Sleeping snuggly, 81

Snacks, 78, 101, 185

Socialization, 25, 27

Sound language, 167

Spaying, 45-46, 51

Special needs, 42

Sprites, 45

STAR*Ferrets, 195

Sterilization, 46

Sterilized, 34

Stress diarrhea, 134

Supplies, 22, 36, 121, 195

Support Our Shelters, 192

Symptoms, 153-154, 160

T

Teeth, 43, 125

Temper tantrums, 156

Temperament, 32, 36-38, 52, 153, 157, 160, 164

Temperature changes, 92

temperature tantrums, 140

Temperature, 193, 41, 148

Ticks, 142

Time, 22

Toilet training, 113

Toys, 23, 25, 26, 63, 89-90, 92, 94-95, 111, 161, 163, 171-
172, 178, 197

Training, 28, 51, 160

aids, 101

deterrents, 101

Tranquilizers, 174

Travel, 25, 173

car, 174

flying, 174

hotel, 175

motel, 175

tips, 177

Traveling, 176

Treats, 78-79, 103, 154, 159, 161

U

Urethral obstruction, 138

V

Vaccinations, 25, 35, 57, 137, 152

Vaccine reactions, 133

Vision, 82

Vocalizing, 77

W

Waardenburg gene, 47

Waardenburg syndrome, 47

Waste management, 117

Water bottle, 61, 89, 114

Water, 23, 26, 60-61, 93, 103, 156, 159

Weaning, 43

Whimpering, 168

Whining, 168

Whiskers, 44

White, 48

Wood shavings, 62

Wounds, 149

Wrestling, 77

Photo Credits